MW00878486

Restoring

THE MINISTRY OF

JESUS

Other Books by Jake Kail

Setting Captives Free

Keys for Deliverance

How to Minister Deliverance Training Manual

Hypocrisy Exposed

Abiding in the Vine

Can a Christian Have a Demon?

Discovering Your Destiny

Kids Empowered Curriculum

Restoring

THE MINISTRY OF

JESUS

How to Walk Like Jesus Walked

JAKE KAIL

Scripture quotations are taken from the New King James Version. Copyright © 1982 by Thomas Nelson, Inc. Used by permission.

Scripture taken from the NEW AMERICAN STANDARD BIBLE®, Copyright © 1960,1962,1963,1968,1971,1972,1973,1975,1977,1995 by The Lockman Foundation. Used by permission.

Scripture quotations marked (ESV) are from The ESV® Bible (The Holy Bible, English Standard Version®), copyright © 2001 by Crossway, a publishing ministry of Good News Publishers. Used by permission. All rights reserved.

Scripture taken from the HOLY BIBLE, NEW INTERNATIONAL VERSION®. NIV®. Copyright© 1973, 1978, 1984 by International Bible Society. Used by permission of Zondervan. All rights reserved.

Copyright © 2022 Jake Kail

Revised and updated edition. Original version published in 2010.

All rights reserved. No part of this publication may be reproduced, stored in a retrieval system, or transmitted in any form or by any means, electronic, mechanical, photocopying, recording, or otherwise, without the prior written permission of the publisher.

ISBN-13: 9798833681909

www.jakekail.com

Dedication

This book is dedicated to those believers who are hungry for *more*. May you receive a fresh passion from the Holy Spirit as you read this book and see the ministry of Jesus alive in your life and church!

Dedication

Acknowledgments

Thank you as always to my wonderful wife, Anna, and our three incredible kids. I appreciate your love and support in all of my writing projects!

Thanks to the Threshold Church family for your hunger for God and willingness to contend to see the ministry of Jesus restored. It is an honor to lead and serve this amazing church body who refuses to settle for the status quo.

A big thanks to the Jake Kail Ministries intercessory prayer team. Thank you for your commitment to praying for me, my family, and this ministry. And thanks for praying for this book project!

Thank you to my assistant, Kate Newcomer, for the time and energy you put into reviewing the rough draft. Thanks for the edits and valuable feedback—this book is better because of you!

Thank you to Erik Berling for designing the cover. I love how it turned out—awesome job!

And most of all, thank you to the Lord Jesus Christ. It is by Your blood that we are redeemed and by Your Spirit that we can walk like You walked and do what You did!

Contents

Introduction

When I was 19 years old, the Lord grabbed a hold of my life in a powerful way. It was at a year-end retreat with a campus ministry following my freshman year in college. Although I had grown up in a wonderful Christian home and had been taught about the gospel, until this time I was not walking in a genuine relationship with God. In this encounter, I experienced a deep work of repentance and instantaneous freedom from bondage to various sinful strongholds. As I turned to God in confession and repentance, His love was tangible, and I wept over His mercy toward me. The direction of my life was drastically changed from that moment on. I became hungry for the things of God. The journey had begun.

Those who know me best know that I tend to be an all-or-nothing kind of guy. Either I am in or I am out, no in between. This tendency had shown up on the sports field, in the classroom, and in personal hobbies. However, somehow it had escaped my Christianity. Up until this encounter, I had lived on the fence with one foot in the world and one in the kingdom of God. I was deceived into thinking that this was okay to the point that I didn't even realize that I was on the fence.

Returning home from this retreat, I was a radically different person. No more double life. No more "faith" without works. No more living in sin. I decided that I would try to read the whole Bible in one year, but I couldn't put it down and actually finished it in three weeks. I was making up for lost time and wasted years that I had spent living for sin and self. God's Word was alive to me, and His voice was coming through each page.

In the early stages of this pursuit of God—which by His grace continues to this day—I started to ask some questions. *Why does the Christianity that I see around me look so different from the ministry of Jesus? Is it possible to experience the Christianity that is portrayed in the Bible? Is the gap between the Bible and church-as-I-know-it our fault or just God's will?* Something told me that there was more to the Christian walk than what I was currently experiencing in my personal life and church expression. Something told me that the ministry of Jesus was supposed to be the ministry of today.

The things that are written in this book are the result of a journey that I have been on for the last several years. I am well aware that I am only scratching the surface of walking in the ministry of Jesus—there is still much ground to be covered, and I continue to press in for more. No doubt there are many others who are much farther ahead of me on this quest. I am thankful for those who have paved the way, sacrificed much, and passed on a legacy to the next generation. I have been positively influenced by many authors and ministers, some of whom have passed away and some who are still alive today.

The subjects discussed in this book are not meant to be comprehensive in nature. There is much more that could be said about many of the topics covered. The intention is to propel readers into a deeper pursuit of God and a greater hunger to see the power of

His kingdom released in the earth today. This book is a call to raise the standard of modern-day ministry so that we will minister like Jesus did. It is a heart cry for revival, restoration, and revolution in the church.

The ministry of Jesus didn't end when He ascended to heaven. It continued on through the apostles and the early church, empowered by the Holy Spirit. The ministry of Jesus is to be the ministry of His people, the church. As His body, we are commissioned to continue His ministry in the earth today. Somewhere along the line we have lowered the standard. Somewhere along the line we have changed the agenda, and the ministry of Jesus ceased to be the norm. This was not God's intention, nor must we settle for it. It is time to restore the ministry of Jesus to the church!

1

What *Did* Jesus Do?

"What would Jesus do?" Do you remember the bracelets that were popular several years ago that had the letters W.W.J.D on them? The idea was that wearing the bracelet would remind a person to make decisions that are Christ-like and to be more like Him. This is certainly an admirable goal. But it seems that for most people, the answer to the question "what would Jesus do?" has only to do with being a generally nice and good person. In other words, when most people talk about following in Christ's footsteps and being like Jesus, they don't look at what He *actually did* and try to imitate it. Activities such as casting out demons or raising the dead certainly never come to mind. Instead, imitating Christ has been reduced to being nice. While kindness is a fruit of the Spirit that we must seek to walk in, niceness and kindness are not always the same. And walking like Jesus is much more than doing our best to be a good and nice person.

During my freshman year in college, I was not walking with the Lord. Though I had been raised in a Christian home and would have considered myself to be a Christian, I was living a deceived lifestyle of sin and selfishness. I remember going to parties and seeing people who were wearing W.W.J.D. bracelets getting drunk and acting like everybody else. Even in the double life that I was living, I realized that something about this did not add up. Wearing the bracelets had become a cheap fad.

The idea of becoming like Christ and walking in His footsteps must go far beyond a popular Christian trend or a humanistic endeavor to be good people. It must become a reality in the church, and it must be based on what the Bible says about Jesus instead of how He is often thought of and portrayed in our society.

What *Did* Jesus Do?

Instead of asking the question "what would Jesus do?" we ought to ask "what *did* Jesus do?" What He *did* do is what He *would* do. So, what is the ministry of Jesus? What did He do?

There are a few times in the gospels where a snapshot summary of Christ's ministry is given. One example is Matthew 4:23-24: "And Jesus went about all Galilee, teaching in their synagogues, preaching the gospel of the kingdom, and healing all kinds of sickness and all kinds of disease among the people. Then His fame went throughout all Syria; and they brought to Him all sick people who were afflicted with various diseases and torments, and those who were demon-possessed, epileptics, and paralytics; and He healed them."

When Jesus first began His public ministry, He stood in a synagogue and quoting from the book of Isaiah said,

"The Spirit of the Lord is upon Me,
  Because He has anointed Me
  To preach the gospel to the poor;
  He has sent Me to heal the brokenhearted,
  To proclaim liberty to the captives
  And recovery of sight to the blind,
  To set at liberty those who are oppressed;
  To proclaim the acceptable year of the Lord."
  (Luke 4:18-19)

This was Jesus' mission statement. He was declaring what He came to the earth to accomplish. Luke 8:1-2 says, "Now it came to pass, afterward, that He went through every city and village, preaching and bringing the glad tidings of the kingdom of God. And the twelve were with Him, and certain women who had been healed of evil spirits and infirmities—Mary called Magdalene, out of whom had come seven demons."

Reading the above passages, as well as other places in the gospels, we see that Jesus' ministry had four basic elements: preaching, teaching, healing, and deliverance. What would Jesus do? He would preach and teach the Word of God with authority in the power of the Holy Spirit. He would cast out demons, heal the sick, and raise the dead. Throughout this book we will talk about each of these four primary ministries and how they must be restored in fullness to the church. However, just as important as the four elements is the motive and heart behind them, so that must be addressed as well.

Though we will go into much more detail later in the book, let's take a brief look at each of the four areas. *Preaching* is a ministry of proclaiming the Word of God, and in Christ's ministry, it was often related to the good news or gospel message. *Teaching*, which is closely related to preaching, is explaining and interpreting the Bible so that people become grounded in the Word. *Healing* ministry is primarily seen as the supernatural restoration of a person's physical body back to health but can also refer to the healing of damaged emotions. *Deliverance* refers to casting out demons in order to set people free from bondage, oppression, and torment.

Just like preaching and teaching are closely related, so are healing and deliverance. Preaching and teaching was the proclamation branch of Christ's ministry while healing and deliverance was the demonstration branch. Both proclamation and demonstration were important to Christ's ministry and both are necessary today. As it says in 1 Corinthians 4:20, "the kingdom of God is not in word but in power." Not only must we teach and preach, we must demonstrate the gospel through healing the sick and casting out demons. If we are to truly carry on the ministry of Jesus, we must preach, teach, heal, and deliver.

A New Creation

Let me suggest to you that Jesus did not die on the cross to only produce a bunch of nice people. He had far more in mind than that. In John 12:24 Jesus said, "Most assuredly, I say to you, unless a grain of wheat falls into the ground and dies, it remains alone; but if it dies, it produces much grain." He was referring to His own death that was about to take place. He was the grain of wheat, or Seed, that was about to fall into the ground and die, and as a result, much fruit would be produced. By God's design, a plant or a tree can only produce fruit according to its own kind (see Genesis 1:11). An apple tree produces more apples; it cannot produce oranges or any other kind of fruit. In the same way, Jesus died on the cross to produce fruit after His own kind: a new breed of human being on the earth that would be like Him, the original Seed.

Second Corinthians 5:17 says, "Therefore, if anyone is in Christ, he is a new creation; old things have passed away; behold, all things have become new." When a person receives Christ, they become a completely new creation and receive a completely new nature. There is a reason that Jesus used the term *born again* when speaking to Nicodemus in John chapter three. The radical nature of the salvation experience demands such a term. It is a creative act of God.

All human beings have inherited a carnal and sinful nature from Adam. At salvation however, this earthly nature is crucified with Christ, and by the Holy Spirit, we become partakers of the divine nature (see 2 Peter 1:3-4). We are taken out of the dominion of darkness and brought into the kingdom of God. We are born again by the incorruptible Seed of the Living Word, Jesus Christ, and by the power of the Holy Spirit. Jesus is called the last Adam, and He came to restore all that the first Adam lost and to reconcile us to the Father. Those who are in Christ are a new creation; they no longer belong to the order of the first Adam, but are now to conform to the image of the last Adam, Christ Jesus. The Seed produces after His own kind.

How is it that we have reduced this glorious gospel to a "get-out-of-hell-free card" or lowered it to a message of self-improvement? Jesus did not die to improve self; He died to replace it. Self cannot be improved, because it is sinful at its core. Instead, it must be put to death and replaced with the nature of Christ. The gospel is not self-help, it is self-denial. Self is not improved, it is crucified. This does not mean that we lose our individual personality or unique identity. On the contrary, we become who God truly created us to be, each one of us a unique expression of His infinite nature.

Do you realize that we are *actually* supposed to be like Jesus? This is not a sentimental idea but a biblical fact. "He who says he abides in Him ought himself also to walk just as He walked" (1 John 2:6). The New Age movement and other false religions have twisted this concept to make people believe that they are equal to Christ or that they become their own god. It is clear that there are ways in which we will never be like Jesus: He is the unique eternal Son of

God, the Messiah, the only Savior who died for our sins, and His name is exalted above every name. Yet it is also clear that there are many ways in which believers are meant to be like Jesus, walk like He walked, and do what He did.

Since this book is about restoring the ministry of Jesus, we will look primarily at how to walk like Jesus as it relates to Christian ministry. However, the teachings and principles that are covered are relevant not only to full-time ministers but to all believers, as we are all called to follow after Jesus.

The Cross and the Spirit

How can we as human beings be expected to walk like Jesus, the perfect Son of God? This cannot happen through human effort or self-improvement. It can only be accomplished through the means which God has provided, the first of which is the cross. Through the power of the cross, our sins are totally forgiven, and we are without guilt or condemnation. This frees us to come into God's presence with confidence and boldness as His children. The penalty for our sin has been paid in full. But not only does the cross take away the penalty of sin, it also takes away the power of sin.

Through the cross, our sinful nature is completely dealt with. Romans 6:6 says that "our old man was crucified with Him, that the body of sin might be done away with, that we should no longer be slaves of sin," and Galatians 5:24 says that "those who are Christ's have crucified the flesh with its passions and desires." Have you considered the fact that you no longer have to be a slave to sin? This is not to say that we will never stumble or that we will never have to battle the flesh; but God has made provision for us to be victorious over sin. We cannot use our human or sinful nature as an excuse for why we are not walking like Jesus.

Until my conversion experience, I never realized that salvation included deliverance from the power of sin. I was aware that Jesus had died for me so that I could be forgiven, but I did not realize that He also wanted to set me free from the controlling grip of sin. The nature of sin is to overpower; it is never satisfied but always wants more control over us. Thank God that through the cross of Jesus Christ we can be delivered from this cruel task-master!

The second means that God has given us is the power of His Spirit. It is not by our own strength but by the power of the Holy Spirit that we can become like Jesus and operate in His ministry. When a person becomes a Christian, the Holy Spirit indwells them and empowers them to live the Christian life. The same Spirit that empowered Jesus for His ministry lives in us. We are not left to our own devices but given the Holy Spirit to be our Helper; and He works to lead us, empower us, and conform us into the image of Jesus.

Earlier I quoted 2 Corinthians 5:17 which says that those who are "in Christ" are a new creation. The key is being in Christ. Being in Christ means that we are identified with Him in His death, resurrection, and ascension. In His death we are delivered from sin. In His resurrection we are empowered with new life. In His ascension we are given authority over the devil, being seated with Him in heavenly places (see Ephesians 2:6).

To be clear, I am not implying that becoming like Christ is an overnight experience. Rather, it is a lifelong pursuit. Second Corinthians 3:18 says that we are being transformed into His image from glory to glory by the power of the Spirit. The problem is not just that we are not walking and ministering like Christ; it is that we do not even see this as a possibility or as the true goal. Like the W.W.J.D. bracelets, we give lip service to the idea but don't really see it as a reality. With the bar of the Christian life lowered, we have no hope of being like Jesus. But if we raise the standard of Christian experience and ministry back to that of the Bible, then we will have hope of walking in this reality.

Our Prophetic Destiny

Throughout my walk with the Lord, I have received prophetic words at different times which have brought much encouragement and strengthening. I remember one time when I was sitting in a small meeting listening to a guest speaker whom I had never met teach about the voice of God. As he was teaching, I began to think about what a father's heart he carried and how I longed to be mentored by someone like him. I had been praying for this type of a mentoring relationship for quite some time. At the end of the meeting, I asked if he would pray for me. As he was praying, he paused and then suddenly began to prophesy to me that God would begin to bring mentors and fathers into my life that would help to shape the course of my ministry and that I was called to be a father to others. This word was such a direct hit that I began to weep uncontrollably.

In another season, I was earnestly seeking God for deeper clarity about the nature of my calling. Some had suggested that I was called to an apostolic ministry, but I wanted to hear from God about this. I went to a conference and during the first day, one of the speakers shared about the apostolic calling. I began to weep as he talked about the cost of walking in this ministry, knowing that God was inviting me to say yes to this. I went to the altar, surrendering to God and saying yes to Him regardless of what it would cost. The very next night at the same conference, another speaker stopped in the middle of his preaching, asked me to stand up, and prophesied over me publicly. Among other significant things, he said, "I see that you will be known as a father. God is releasing a great apostolic anointing over your life..." Again I wept as the Lord was so clearly speaking and confirming His call upon my life.

A prophetic word is oftentimes a declaration of God's destiny for a person. But no matter how accurate or powerful a prophet is, none can compare to Jesus. Did you know that Jesus has prophesied over you? Consider the following Scripture: "Most assuredly, I say to you, *he who believes in Me*, the works that I do he will do also; and greater works than these he will do, because I go to My Father" (John 14:12, emphasis added). If you are a believer in Jesus, this verse applies to you. *Jesus prophesied that you and I would do the same works that He did and even greater works.*

One more example is from Mark 16:17-18 (emphasis added): "And these signs will follow *those who believe*: In My name they will cast out demons...they will lay hands on the sick, and they will recover." These again are the words of Jesus and apply to "those who believe" which includes you and me. Jesus prophesied that we would cast out demons and heal the sick. We must take these words personally and apply them to ourselves. When I read the above verses, I see them as a personal prophetic word from Jesus to me. According to Jesus, I will do the same works that He did.

Jesus is recognized as the Messiah because of the many Old Testament prophecies that He fulfilled. Could we be recognized as His disciples according to the above prophecies made concerning us? Like Paul told Timothy, we need to wage the good warfare with these prophetic words of Jesus until they become a reality in our lives (see 1 Timothy 1:18). Our prophetic destiny is to be like Jesus.

Apart from the finished work of the cross and the power of the Holy Spirit, we could never be expected to walk like Jesus walked, do what Jesus did, and continue to minister as Jesus ministered. But we are not without the cross or the Holy Spirit and therefore we are without excuse. The church is to continue the full ministry of Jesus in the earth. Some recognize this and seek to restore what has been lost. Some find excuses to maintain the status quo of the hour. The second choice is simply not an option for me. I burn to see the ministry of Jesus fully restored and functioning in His church!

2

Contending for the Promised Land

Jesus is the model for the Christian life and for true Christian ministry. I submit to you that as the church of Jesus Christ, we are currently living far below the standard of God's Word. To demonstrate this, let's look at the following passage of Scripture.

> But if the ministry of death, written and engraved on stones, was glorious, so that the children of Israel could not look steadily at the face of Moses because of the glory of his countenance, which glory was passing away, how will the ministry of the Spirit not be more glorious? For if the ministry of condemnation had glory, the ministry of righteousness exceeds much more in glory. For even what was made glorious had no glory in this respect, because of the glory that excels. For if what is passing away was

glorious, what remains is much more glorious. (2 Corinthians 3:7-11)

I encourage you to take a careful look at this passage. As we know, Moses walked in a powerful realm of the glory of God. But Paul is saying that compared to what we now possess, Moses had nothing. The ministry of the Spirit under the new covenant is to be far more glorious than the glory that Moses experienced under the old. We look back at Moses with jealousy at His experience with God, while Paul says that we should have much more. Clearly, we have some ground to recover—we are living far beneath God's intent!

Restoring the ministry of Jesus is actually nothing more than walking in the fullness of the promises that God has given to us in His Word. In other words, if we were walking in the totality of God's promises, we would be demonstrating the life and ministry of Christ in its entirety. It is essential that we understand and obtain the things that God has promised to us as His children. We will talk more specifically about those promises later in this chapter, but first I want to lay a proper foundation for receiving them.

Throughout His Word, God has spoken many promises to His people. A misunderstanding of how these promises are received has caused many to miss out on living in their reality. We tend to think that God's promises automatically happen, but this is not the case according to the Bible. His promises require human involvement and partnership. Let's look at the Promised Land of the Old Testament as an illustration of this.

The Promised Land

When God made His covenant with Abraham, Isaac, and Jacob, He promised to give them a land of their own where their descendants would live and flourish. When Moses brought the children of

Israel out of Egypt after four hundred years of slavery, they were to finally see the fulfillment of this promise. Before going in to take possession of this land, Moses sent out twelve spies to check out the nature of the land, the people, and the cities and to bring back some of its fruit (see Numbers 13:1-20). This spying out of the land was ordained by God and was accompanied by a reminder of the promise: "And the Lord spoke to Moses, saying, 'Send men to spy out the land of Canaan, *which I am giving to the children of Israel*; from each tribe of their fathers you shall send a man, every one a leader among them'" (Numbers 13:1-2, emphasis added).

After forty days the spies returned with this report: "We went to the land where you sent us. It truly flows with milk and honey, and this is its fruit. Nevertheless the people who dwell in the land are strong; the cities are fortified and very large; moreover we saw the descendants of Anak there. The Amalekites dwell in the land of the South; the Hittites, the Jebusites, and the Amorites dwell in the mountains; and the Canaanites dwell by the sea and along the banks of the Jordan" (Numbers 13:27-29). Caleb, also one of the twelve spies, tried to encourage the people to go in and take the land but instead the negative report continued: "We are not able to go up against the people, for they are stronger than we" (verse 31).

Only two of the spies, Joshua and Caleb, were confident that they could go in and take possession of this land that God had promised them. The negative report of the other ten spies turned the whole nation of Israel into an upheaval to the point of rebelling against Moses and even wanting to return to Egypt. The Lord then determined that this whole generation would have to wander in the desert for the next forty years where they would eventually die, never entering into the land that was promised to them. Of that generation, only Joshua and Caleb would be able to see the fulfillment of the promise.

Because of fear and unbelief, the children of Israel failed to receive the clear promise of God. They wanted the promise without the fight. They didn't realize that they were going to have to contend for the Promised Land, so when they saw the enemy, they retreated. They preferred the safety (and bondage) of Egypt to the danger (and freedom) of the land that "flowed with milk and honey."

Forty years later after Moses had died and after the rebellious generation who refused the promises of God had passed away in the wilderness, the Lord spoke to Joshua and gave him this commission: "Moses My servant is dead. Now therefore, arise, go over this Jordan, you and all this people, *to the land which I am giving to them*—the children of Israel. Every place that the sole of your foot will tread upon I have given you, as I said to Moses" (Joshua 1:2-3, emphasis added). Again, the commission is given and the promise reiterated. This time the people followed through, and after crossing the Jordan River they began to take possession of the land of promise one section at a time.

In this example and throughout the whole Bible, we can see that the promises of God do not automatically happen. His promises are an invitation to partner with Him in prayer and obedience to see them fulfilled. They are not a free pass to passively sit by but an invitation to contend in faith.

Our Spiritual Inheritance

This story of entering the Promised Land has tremendous implications for us today. It teaches us that the promises of God are not automatic but conditional. We too have a promised land, a spiritual inheritance from the Lord, and if we are going to enter it, we will have to contend for it. It will not happen by itself and like the children of Israel, we can choose not to enter into it. *Each generation must decide if they will take possession of the land or settle for a substitute.*

Our general spiritual inheritance is comprised of all of the promises that God has made to us in His Word. Every believer also has a personal promised land of all of the promises and prophetic words they have received from God. For our purposes, I want to look at three categories of promises from the Bible that relate to walking in the ministry of Jesus.

1. The Promise of Intimacy

Jesus walked in incredible intimacy with the Father. In fact, His whole ministry flowed out of that intimate relationship. Jesus Himself said, "Most assuredly, I say to you, the Son can do nothing of Himself, but what He sees the Father do; for whatever He does, the Son also does in like manner. For the Father loves the Son, and shows Him all things that He Himself does" (John 5:19-20). Jesus walked with the Father and was led continually by the Holy Spirit.

When Jesus died on the cross, He made the way for us to have an intimate relationship with God. The veil of the temple was torn, giving us immediate access to His presence through the blood of Christ. We can now draw near to God knowing that we are completely forgiven and develop a true, personal relationship with Him. If we are going to walk in the ministry of Jesus, we must make intimacy with God our highest priority. It is the root system from which everything else grows.

Let's look at a few promises from the Bible about this intimate relationship.

> I am the good shepherd; and I know My sheep, and am known by My own...My sheep hear My voice, and I know them, and they follow Me. (John 10:14, 27)

> He who has My commandments and keeps them, it is he who loves Me. And he who loves Me will be loved by My Father, and I will love him and manifest Myself to him. (John 14:21)

God has promised to reveal Himself to us as we walk in obedience to His commands. He has promised to lead us and guide us as a shepherd guides his sheep. We are to know God and become familiar with His voice; this is our spiritual inheritance.

2. The Promise of Character

The second category of promises is character. We know that Jesus was perfect in character and lived without sin. If we are going to truly exhibit the ministry of Jesus today, we will have to do more than move in mighty acts of power. Along with demonstrating His power to heal and deliver, we must display His nature: His holiness, love, goodness, patience, humility, and compassion. Without this corresponding character, we will not make it for the long haul.

Thankfully, part of our spiritual promised land includes the promise of Christ's character and nature in us.

> His divine power has given to us all things that pertain to life and godliness, through the knowledge of Him who called us by glory and virtue, by which have been given to us exceedingly great and precious promises, that through these you may be partakers of the divine nature, having escaped the corruption that is in the world through lust. (2 Peter 1:3-4)

This passage says that through the great and precious promises of God, we can partake of God's nature. That is a powerful thought! We are no longer to be controlled by the sinful nature but are to progressively be transformed into the image of Christ from glory to glory (see 2 Corinthians 3:18).

3. The Promise of Power

The third category of promises that belong to us in Christ are promises relating to power. Jesus operated in tremendous power.

Acts 10:38 says that "God anointed Jesus of Nazareth with the Holy Spirit and with power, who went about doing good and healing all who were oppressed by the devil, for God was with Him." If Jesus needed to be empowered by the Holy Spirit to fulfill His ministry, how much more do we? We must not settle for ministering in our own strength and human wisdom. Here are a few promises relating to power for life and ministry.

> But you shall receive power when the Holy Spirit has come upon you; and you shall be witnesses to Me in Jerusalem, and in all Judea and Samaria, and to the end of the earth. (Acts 1:8)

> Most assuredly, I say to you, he who believes in Me, the works that I do he will do also; and greater works than these he will do, because I go to My Father. (John 14:12)

Compared to the promises that God has made to us, the power of the Holy Spirit is embarrassingly absent in most of our churches today. Where are the powerful healings and miracles of the Bible? The power of God was so strong in the early church that people were healed by Peter's shadow and Paul's handkerchief. Where is Peter's shadow or Paul's handkerchief today? I say this not to condemn but to inspire. There is more to contend for!

Restoration of the Land

The above passages are but a brief sampling of the promises that God has given to us. I mention them for the purpose of spying out our promised land and tasting some of its fruit. The question is, will you choose to enter in and contend for the fullness of these promises to come into being in your life? Remember, the promises of God are not automatic.

I have personally found that most believers seem fairly content to remain outside the promised land of their inheritance. Like the

Israelites of old, we can find a plethora of excuses as to why we are not willing to take possession of the fullness of all that Christ has purchased for us. For some it is an ignorance of what the promises are. For others it is an unbelief that we can actually enter in or an unwillingness to pay the price of contending. And for others it is a theological belief system that lowers the biblical standard to our present level of experience. As a result, much Christian ministry today does not resemble the ministry of Jesus and much church-life looks nothing like the book of Acts.

Even in the midst of all of this, God is restoring His church to its original power and glory. Over the last five centuries, there has been a progressive process of restoring everything that was lost during the dark ages of the church. In the days of Martin Luther, the promise of *intimacy* was restored through the doctrines of justification by faith and the priesthood of all believers. In the time of John Wesley, the promise of *character* was restored with the doctrine of sanctification. In the Azusa Street revival of the early 1900s, the promise of *power* was restored with the outpouring of the Spirit and the doctrine of the baptism of the Holy Spirit. These are just a few of the examples of the truths that God is restoring His church.

But God is interested in more than simply restoring truths and doctrines to His people. He wants to restore His glory. The process of restoration that has been occurring is about restoring the life and ministry of Jesus to the church. It is about the church becoming the glorious bride that it is meant to be. It is about restoring the church to a place where Jesus is truly the Head, and we as His body are accurately representing Him in the earth.

There are two dangers that we must be careful to avoid in our quest for restoration. The first danger is to camp out at one place of revelation and not move on to the next. God's restoration process is progressive and we must be willing to move with the cloud so to speak. Some have camped out at Luther's revelation of justification by faith, some at Wesley's doctrine of sanctification, and others at the Azusa Street revival. The problem with this is that none of these movements have the whole picture, and God still has more to restore. We must be willing to continue to move on with God as He brings new light to the church.

The second danger is to move on to the next stage of restoration while forgetting the previous ones. When we go from one step of revelation to the next, we are not to leave the previous one behind but to build upon it. For example, if you teach the doctrine of sanctification without the doctrine of justification you will end up with legalism. Sanctification must build upon the already established truth that we are saved by grace through faith alone and are already completely accepted and loved by God because of the cross.

I sometimes worry that in new movements of the Holy Spirit we teach the present emphasis of God but leave out the proper foundation on which it is built. The result is a shallow version of what God truly intended. One need only to compare the books of classic Christian authors to what is popular in today's Christian bookstore to see this truth. But how powerful would it be if we took the revelations that God is presently teaching us and built them upon the depth of the life in Christ that A.W. Tozer, Andrew Murray, or other classic writers walked in?

The revelations and teachings that God wants to restore today including signs, wonders, and creative miracles will only fully benefit the church when they are properly placed in the building under the proper foundation. As you forge ahead, do not forget your roots.

Even with these and other dangers, we must move forward and contend for our promised land to be restored. There is no other valid option. We must seek God for His promises to come to pass in our lives instead of making excuses for not walking in them.

Don't Settle for a Substitute

Rehoboam was the son of Solomon and reigned after Solomon died. In his days as king, judgment came upon Israel because of their idolatry. Let's read the account told in 1 Kings 14:25-26:

> It happened in the fifth year of King Rehoboam that Shi-shak king of Egypt came up against Jerusalem. And he took away the treasures of the house of the Lord and the treasures of the king's house; he took away everything. He also took away all the gold shields which Solomon had made.

An enemy nation actually entered into the house of God and stole of its treasures, including the gold shields that Solomon had made. Look at the response of King Rehoboam in the next verse: "Then King Rehoboam made bronze shields in their place" (1 Kings 14:27). Instead of going after the gold shields, he created a cheap substitute. This is a great illustration of the church today. The enemy has stolen our gold—our power, effectiveness, and overall glory—and instead of contending for our inheritance we have by and large settled for a cheap substitute.

Saints, we have two options. We can go after all that God has given us and see the ministry of Jesus restored, or we can settle for bronze shields. We have to contend for our promised land, not because God is reluctant to give it to us, but because we have an enemy who vehemently opposes us and loves to rob us of our full inheritance. Joshua once asked a question to seven of the tribes of Israel. Let's allow this question to spur us on to pursue and possess our spiritual promised land: "How long will you neglect to go and possess the land which the Lord God of your fathers has given you?" (Joshua 18:3). We have no time to waste. It's time to contend!

3

Spirit-Empowered Preaching

As stated previously, one of the four primary activities of Christ's ministry was preaching. We desperately need a revival of authentic, Spirit-empowered preaching in our day. Jesus was not a motivational speaker, and I think we in the church would do well to leave the motivational speaking and self-help methods to the business arena. Jesus was a preacher and to preach is to proclaim the Word of God with authority and power. This type of preaching is very rare today, as it also was in the days of Jesus (see Matthew 7:28-29). We have many gifted communicators and entertaining sermonizers, but where are the ones sent by God who can release the Word in the power of the Holy Spirit? Where are the ones whose words are on fire and draw people to repentance, encounters with God, and radical transformation?

The Danger of Soulish Preaching

It seems that preparing and delivering sermons has become a science these days—it can be so calculated. If we say the right things, at the right time, and in the right way, we can expect a certain response from the congregation. Instead of aiming for true transformation, we often preach to get a momentary reaction from the crowd. Whether we want to acknowledge it or not, much preaching today, and ministry in general for that matter, is aimed at the soul instead of the spirit. The long-term effects of this soulish Christianity produce little lasting fruit.

Here is what I mean. Human beings are made up of three primary parts: body, soul, and spirit (see 1 Thessalonians 5:23). The human soul consists of the mind, will, and emotions. The human spirit, after being born again, is the aspect of our being that is able to fellowship with God and grow up in Him. When I say that much of today's preaching is being aimed at the human soul instead of the spirit, I mean that it is primarily affecting the intellect or emotions but not penetrating to the spirit.

Preaching that is aimed at the mind increases head knowledge without reaching the heart. This does not build up the spirit or draw people into a deeper intimacy with the Lord but instead "puffs up" (see 1 Corinthians 8:1). Preaching that is aimed at the emotions may stir people for a moment, but after the message is over, it is business as usual. So, while preaching to the mind brings *information* and preaching to the emotions brings *inspiration*, neither produce lasting *transformation*. The results of these types of preaching are devastating because the people of God do not get the spiritual nourishment that they need. Meanwhile, since the soul has been stimulated, there is a false sense of spiritual fulfillment similar to when a baby with a pacifier forgets that he is hungry. *Soulish preaching pacifies, but it doesn't feed.*

Ministering to the soul instead of to the spirit has become a cheap substitute in the body of Christ. Our meetings are reduced to emotional pep rallies full of hype on one side and dry intellectual forums on the other. Neither of these types of meetings necessitates the presence of God. I am concerned that much of what is called anointed today in regards to worship or preaching is probably nothing more than a manufactured manipulation of emotions.

Obviously, the mind and the emotions are important parts of the human make-up, and I am not in any way suggesting that we neglect them; only that we put them in their proper place. Information is good and so is inspiration, but they alone will not get the job done. What is needed to reach the human spirit is the true Word of God, anointed by the Holy Spirit and proclaimed with authority. This has nothing to do with using a certain preaching style or having a certain type of personality. It is a matter of heart, motives, and true spiritual substance. Spirit-empowered preaching flows from a life that is consecrated to God and full of the Holy Spirit.

The Message of Jesus

Another essential element for restoring the complete ministry of Jesus is restoring the message of Jesus. What was the message that Jesus preached? Matthew 4:23 says that Jesus went throughout Galilee "preaching the gospel of the kingdom." Let's also look at Mark 1:14-15: "Now after John was put in prison, Jesus came to Galilee, preaching the gospel of the kingdom of God, and saying, 'The time is fulfilled, and the kingdom of God is at hand. Repent, and believe in the gospel.'" This is the same message that John the Baptist preached. John was the forerunner of Christ and paved the way for His ministry. Spirit-empowered preaching with a call for repentance opens the way for Christ's ministry to operate.

There must be a shift in our message. Not only did Jesus preach the gospel of salvation, He preached the gospel of the kingdom, and it is critical that we see the difference. The gospel of salvation basically says, "Believe in Jesus so that when you die you will go to heaven." Growing up, this was my understanding of the gospel. Jesus died on the cross so that I could be forgiven and have eternal life if I would believe in Him. Though there is certainly truth in this, it is not the complete picture. Rather, it is only a part of the gospel that Jesus preached. If we reduce the gospel to this message, it will severely limit the full ministry of Jesus.

So, what's the difference between the gospel of salvation and the gospel of the kingdom? The gospel of salvation emphasizes Jesus as *Savior*. The gospel of the kingdom emphasizes Jesus as *Lord*. The gospel of salvation speaks of freedom from the *penalty* of sin. The gospel of the kingdom speaks of freedom from the *power* of sin. The gospel of salvation aims to produce *converts*. The gospel of the kingdom aims to produce *disciples*. The gospel of salvation is about *escaping*. The gospel of the kingdom is about *advancing*. It is not so much a matter of semantics but of substance. In other words, it is not about simply changing what we call the gospel. Like Jesus, we must preach the message of the kingdom of God in its entirety.

In saying these things, I am not implying that these two messages are in opposition to each other. The gospel of salvation must be preached as a part of the overall gospel of the kingdom, but not as the entire message itself. God certainly wants people to be saved and have eternal life, but the gospel is broader than this. For example, preaching only the gospel of salvation excludes the message and ministry of physical healing and deliverance from demons. These are vital elements of the gospel of the kingdom but are lost when the gospel of salvation is the only focus. Again, these messages are not opposed to each other. But to restore the ministry of Jesus, we must restore the message of Jesus. Let's unpack this message a bit more.

The Kingdom – God's Revolution

Jesus came to establish and advance God's kingdom—His rule and reign, or lordship—on the earth. He did not come only to bring people from earth to heaven; He came to bring heaven to earth. The kingdom of heaven is God's revolution being launched on the earth. It calls for a complete revolt against sin and this world system that is under the control of the evil one and total allegiance to Jesus Christ as King.

One definition for the word *revolution* is "the complete overthrow of one government and its replacement with another." Another definition is "a radical and pervasive change in society and the social structure." When Jesus said, "The time is fulfilled, and the kingdom of God is at hand," He was saying that heaven's revolution had begun. His kingdom was here to overthrow and replace the kingdom (or government) of darkness, and as a result there would be a dramatic and all-consuming change in society. If we try to change society without overthrowing the spiritual forces that are controlling it, we will not succeed at producing any lasting fruit. But when the kingdom of God overthrows the powers of darkness, you can be sure that society will be changed.

By saying that God's kingdom was at hand Jesus was saying that Satan's reign of terror was over. The kingdom of darkness is characterized by sin, sickness, torment, and fear. The kingdom of light is characterized by salvation, healing, deliverance, and faith. What Satan had gained through the fall of man Jesus had come to reclaim.

Let me summarize it like this. God created man and gave him dominion over the earth. Man sinned, coming into agreement with the serpent and joining him in his rebellion. What we sometimes do not realize is that when man sinned, he gave his God-given authority over the earth to the devil. This is why Jesus called Satan the "ruler of the world" and why Paul called him the "god of this age" (see John 14:30, 2 Corinthians 4:4). Through His death and resurrection, Jesus reclaimed this authority and has given it to the church.

Immediately after declaring that the kingdom of God was at hand, Jesus gave a call to repentance (see Mark 1:14-15). Sin empowers the devil's kingdom and therefore repentance undermines it. The devil is defeated, and he knows that the only way he can gain control of people's lives is when they agree with him. Sin is agreement with the devil and enables him to have authority over areas of our lives. Repentance from sin and faith in Jesus not only bring salvation but also make the way for God's kingdom to invade our lives and ultimately the world around us. The gospel is meant to restore us to a right relationship with God and at the same time to release His kingdom in the earth.

The message of the kingdom is absolutely essential to restoring the ministry of Jesus to the church. It is the foundation for everything that Jesus did. He healed the sick and cast out demons, because the kingdom of God was at hand. We need a renewal of the mind as to just what exactly the gospel entails. It is not simply about securing people a place in heaven and then teaching them principles of "spiritual growth" which usually add up to ways of improving their lives. It is about the kingdom of heaven invading the earth and bringing everything under the authority of the King. God wants us saved and living in eternal life. We should certainly desire His rulership on earth as it is in heaven.

Motives and Methods

In order to restore the ministry of Jesus, we will not only have to restore the message of Jesus but also the motives of Jesus. Our motivation for preaching should be obedience to God and the true transformation of people's lives. When we change our objective from pleasing God and transforming lives to pleasing people and keeping them happy, we have just taken a dangerous step away from the ministry of Jesus.

Jesus did not preach to please people. He was not swayed by popular opinion and did not water down His message to make it "seeker-sensitive." Jesus was not concerned when crowds of people stopped following Him, because he was not controlled by numbers (see John 6:60-66). He did not measure success by the amount of people following Him but by obedience to the Father. We need to get this into our hearts and minds: *obedience equals success.* I fear that there is a major over-emphasis on numerical growth today in the Western church system. As a result, the appearance of success has taken the place of lasting fruit. Consider the following passage.

> And seeing from afar a fig tree having leaves, He went to see if perhaps He would find something on it. When He came to it, He found nothing but leaves, for it was not the season for figs. (Mark 11:13)

From a distance the fig tree looked promising; it had the appearance of success. But upon closer examination, it was barren. Could this also be the case in many of our churches? When a church is seeing rapid numerical growth, it appears to be succeeding, but numerical growth does not equal fruit. When we stand at the Judgment Seat of Christ it will be the quality, not quantity, of our work that is tested (see 1 Corinthians 3:13-15).

I am not necessarily opposed to fast numerical growth or to big churches, but large numbers of people do not automatically mean fruitfulness. Fruit is not determined by how many people are attending a church but by what is being produced in the lives of those people. Think of the number of people as trees, not fruit. A church can have many "trees," but if they are like the above fig tree—without fruit—then we have missed the point. Week after week, multitudes of people are sitting in our pews and not receiving the ministry that they so desperately need: the true ministry of Jesus which includes Spirit-led and Spirit-empowered preaching. We make a mistake when we assume that people will just eventually get it if we can keep them coming back to our churches. Let's remember that church members are not customers to be kept or consumers to be entertained but saints to be equipped. Have we turned the Father's house into a marketplace?

Jesus did not sell the gospel, and He did not make it easy. He told people to count the cost. The rich young ruler came to Jesus and asked Him what he must do to inherit eternal life. Jesus looked at him with love and then told him to sell his possessions, give the money to the poor, take up his cross, and follow Him (see Mark 10:17-22). Apparently, loving the rich young ruler meant calling him to full consecration and devotion to Jesus. But the young man declined; he sadly wanted heaven but not Jesus.

What if a "rich young ruler" walked into a church today and asked the same question? I have a feeling we might answer in a different way than Jesus did. He's the kind of person you want to keep around, not drive away. He is influential. If he joins the church, surely others in the community will notice and follow. He is also wealthy and could be the key to a successful building campaign. Has our desire to attract people caused us to compromise the message and use methods that are less than pure?

Isaac or Ishmael?

Impure motives lead to man-made methods; and man-made methods can only produce man-made results. I often wonder if some of our modern preaching and church growth methods are producing Isaacs or Ishmaels. In the story of Abraham found in Genesis 15-21, God gave him a promise that he would have a son even though he and his wife were well past the age of producing children. Instead of believing the promise as it was given, his wife

Sarai (later called Sarah), suggested that he sleep with her maidservant Hagar. The result was Ishmael.

Ishmael represents the product of the flesh, human effort, while Isaac is called the child of promise born "by the power of the Spirit" (Galatians 4:29 NIV). Ishmael and Isaac had a lot in common. They may have looked similar, talked the same, and in some ways acted the same, but their destinies were worlds apart. We have to honestly ask ourselves if we are producing converts by the power of the Spirit or by human tactics and effort. When we resort to worldly methods, we unite with Hagar. When a Spirit-filled church embraces the seeker-sensitive model of church growth, Abraham marries Hagar, and Ishmael is born.

Commercialism comes into our ministry when we become more concerned with attracting people than equipping people and give more priority to pleasing man than to pleasing God. It is God Himself that we should want to attract; who cares how many people show up if God's presence does not? Preaching that is aimed at the soul instead of the spirit, and preaching that is designed to please people will end up producing Ishmaels instead of Isaacs. I am not saying that no good will be done or that no one will truly be saved, but it will certainly be far from God's best.

The type of preaching that I am referring to falls short because it ignores spiritual realities, neglects the power of God, and dilutes true Christianity. It is time to leave human methods behind and preach the Word of God with the anointing of the Spirit. Spirit-empowered preaching is so important to restoring the ministry of Jesus, because it will set the tone and overall spiritual atmosphere needed for the other three elements of His ministry to operate. Remember, it was the preaching of the message of repentance and the message of the kingdom of God through John the Baptist and then through Jesus Himself that paved the way for His ministry on earth.

Preaching the Word

For the word of God is living and powerful, and sharper than any two-edged sword, piercing even to the division of soul and spirit, and of joints and marrow, and is a discerner of the thoughts and intents of the heart. (Hebrews 4:12)

Do you realize that it is possible to preach a doctrinally sound sermon and not have preached the Word of God? There is a difference between a biblical message and the Word of the Lord. I am not referring necessarily to the gift of prophecy but to preaching the Word by the power and direction of the Spirit. For example, if I preach a biblically accurate message on the love of God when the Lord wanted me to speak on the fear of God (or vice versa), I have missed the mark; the message was biblical but was not the Word of God for that day.

I am not saying that every message we preach must come as a direct revelation from God on what topic to choose or passage to preach from. But if we are sincerely seeking God, we should begin to pick up on His heart and learn to be led by Him in our preaching. If what we had planned to preach is not in line with His heart, we need to be sensitive enough to the Spirit to change the direction of the message. In other words, preaching should not be mechanical. Some pastors have a whole year's worth of messages planned out in advance and just go right through without seeking the heart of God. Others preach from online resources or other people's messages and books without considering the leading of the Spirit.

I believe that God wants to bring us to the point where our whole life is a message. We are seeking God and meeting with Him in the secret place, living a life pleasing to Him, and walking in the Spirit on a daily basis. His Word is becoming flesh in us. When we preach, it is an outflow of our relationship with God and an overflow of the work of the Holy Spirit. Our messages are coming from the throne of God and they carry a weightiness. We are listening to the Lord and are flexible to change our message at the last minute because of the Holy Spirit's direction. God has been stretching me in this area recently, and I have found myself preaching without notes and sometimes without any pre-planned message. It's not about how a person prepares sermons or whether or not they use notes, but somehow we have to get away from mechanical and formulaic preaching and into Spirit-empowered preaching.

Preaching is meant to have a prophetic anointing to it that carries with it a sense of God's heart and mind for the hour. While it is essential that our messages are biblical, biblical messages alone are not enough. In fact, biblical messages void of God's Spirit are destroying God's people because they have replaced the living Word of God anointed by the Spirit. This may sound harsh, but Paul said that the "letter kills, but the Spirit gives life" (2 Corinthians 3:6). Restoring the ministry of Jesus means restoring the living Word of the Lord. We can no longer afford to be satisfied with doctrinally sound sermons that don't produce lasting fruit.

Demonstration

Jesus not only preached the Word, He also demonstrated it through acts of power, healings, and deliverances. This was also the pattern of the early church.

> Then Philip went down to the city of Samaria and *preached* Christ to them. And the multitudes with one accord heeded the things spoken by Philip, *hearing and seeing* the miracles which he did. For unclean spirits, crying with a loud voice, came out of many who were possessed; and many who were paralyzed and lame were healed. (Acts 8:5-7, emphasis added)

The gospel is meant to be both heard and seen. Proclamation without demonstration is not the full ministry of Jesus. That is why Paul said, "And my speech and my preaching were not with persuasive words of human wisdom, but in demonstration of the Spirit and of power, that your faith should not be in the wisdom of men but in the power of God" (1 Corinthians 2:4-5). Signs and wonders are meant to accompany and confirm the preaching of God's Word. Signs follow Jesus, so if we are close enough to Him, they should begin to follow us as well.

We will take a look at healing and deliverance—the two main ways that Jesus demonstrated the Word—in later chapters. But first, let's explore the second of Christ's four main ministries which is closely related to preaching; and that is the ministry of teaching.

4

The Ministry of Teaching

One of the most common titles given to Jesus in the gospels was Teacher, because one of His most common activities was to teach. "And Jesus went about all Galilee, teaching in their synagogues…" (Matthew 4:23). "Then He went about the villages in a circuit, teaching" (Mark 6:6). Jesus taught in the temple, taught in the synagogues, and taught in homes. He also taught outdoors, on a mountain, in the wilderness, and in the marketplace.

When people heard Jesus teach, they noticed something different about Him. "And they were astonished at His teaching, for He taught them as one having authority, and not as the scribes" (Mark 1:22). Jesus taught with authority. He explained and interpreted the Scriptures in ways that the people had never heard before. He spoke with certainty; there was no second guessing in His words.

Obviously, there was a big difference between the way that Jesus and the scribes taught, so much so that the people were astonished.

While preaching is a ministry of *proclaiming* truth, teaching primarily relates to *explaining* truth. The basic principles that I mentioned in the previous chapter on preaching certainly apply to teaching as well. But teaching has a specific purpose to it that makes it different than preaching.

The Purpose of Teaching

One of the most famous passages to record the teaching ministry of Jesus is what is known as the Sermon on the Mount found in Matthew 5-7. The very last section of this sermon tells us the intended result of His teaching.

> Therefore whoever hears these sayings of Mine, and does them, I will liken him to a wise man who built his house on the rock: and the rain descended, the floods came, and the winds blew and beat on that house; and it did not fall, for it was founded on the rock. But everyone who hears these sayings of Mine, and does not do them, will be like a foolish man who built his house on the sand: and the rain descended, the floods came, and the winds blew and beat on that house; and it fell. And great was its fall. (Matthew 7:24-27)

The purpose of teaching is to ground people in the Word of God. In order for this to occur, two things are needed: proper teaching and proper response to that teaching. Let's first assume that the teaching is proper and in line with the ministry of Jesus and Word of God. Jesus would then liken the person who hears and does His words to a wise man who built a solid foundation for the house he was building. Because his house was built upon a solid foundation, it was able to endure when a strong storm came through. On the other hand, the person who hears His words but does not put them into practice is compared to a foolish man who built a house on a weak foundation. The same storm that the wise man's house withstood toppled the house of the foolish man.

If you were to have looked at these two houses from the outside, they would have appeared the same. Not until the storm came was the true character of each house revealed. The same is true in our lives. Take for example two fictional characters named Bill and John. Both go to the same church and sit under the same teaching every week. Bill listens to each message with an earnest spirit and puts the truths that he is hearing into practice. He also spends regular time reading God's Word on his own, letting it sink into his heart and impact the way he lives. John on the other hand pays little attention as his pastor is teaching and once the message is over, he goes on with life. He rarely reads the Bible and doesn't seem too interested in what it has to say.

Day by day Bill is laying a solid foundation for his life while John is building his "house on the sand." From the outside nobody would be able to tell the difference. Both attend church regularly and both seem to possess God's love and joy. But when the storms of life come into their lives, the difference becomes apparent. Bill maintains an attitude of peace and trust in the Lord while John panics and becomes angry at God. Bill's life remains intact while John's falls apart.

In this life storms are inevitable. There is no avoiding them, only enduring them. Storms may come in various ways, shapes, and sizes but you can be sure that they will come. When the storm hits, it is too late to build the foundation. Though the wise builder in Jesus' story had to take the extra time, effort, and energy to lay the proper foundation for his home, in the end it paid off royally. Jesus said that in this world we would have trouble. If our lives are built upon the rock, we will be able to take heart knowing that He has overcome the world (see John 16:33).

When hurricane Katrina hit New Orleans in 2005, my wife and I were living in a small Louisiana town about sixty miles away. Althhough the damage in our area was not nearly as devastating as it was in New Orleans, the effects of the storm could be clearly seen. It was amazing to see trees completely uprooted from the ground. The interesting thing was that in the same yard would be trees that were perfectly intact. The same storm that uprooted one tree left another unharmed. What was the difference between the two? One was firmly rooted and the other was not.

The importance of being rooted in God's Word must not be underestimated. Though we often want to soar in the Spirit, it is equally important to be grounded in the Word. As stated above, this comes from proper teaching coupled with the appropriate response of putting the teaching into action. It certainly must also come from spending time alone with God, meditating on His Word. Consider Psalm 1:1-3:

> Blessed is the man
> Who walks not in the counsel of the ungodly,
> Nor stands in the path of sinners,
> Nor sits in the seat of the scornful;
> But his delight is in the law of the Lord,
> And in His law he meditates day and night.
> He shall be like a tree
> Planted by the rivers of water,
> That brings forth its fruit in its season,
> Whose leaf also shall not wither;
> And whatever he does shall prosper.

Effective Teaching

If we want people to become grounded in the truths of Scripture, then we have a responsibility to give them proper and effective teaching. Whether or not people decide to put the teaching into practice is outside of our control; our job is to teach soundly. Because of the important nature of teaching, James says that those who teach will be judged more strictly (see James 3:1). We ought to take that warning seriously and strive to teach with purity and effectiveness. Below are some of the qualities that make up effective teaching.

Teaching with Authority

As we have already seen, when Jesus taught, the people noticed that His teaching carried an authority with it that was lacking in the teaching of the scribes and Pharisees. Have you ever noticed that some teachers just seem to have an authority in their voice? When they speak people listen, and there is a weightiness to what is said. Two people can say the same words or teach the same basic message but produce totally different results depending on the level of authority that each one carries.

There is no substitute for this type of authority and anointing and it is not something that can be learned. It comes from a deep relationship with God and a revelation of His Word. When you stand in the presence of God and His Word becomes a reality in your life, then you will truly experience and believe what you teach and your words will carry weight.

Getting to the Spirit of the Law

Jesus did not simply teach the letter of the law, He got to the spirit of the Law. The letter refers to the actual words on the page and the spirit refers to the purpose and motive behind the words. While the letter of the law impacts outward behavior, the spirit of the law cuts to the heart. Let's look at one example to illustrate this point.

> You have heard that it was said to those of old, 'You shall not commit adultery.' But I say to you that whoever looks at a woman to lust for her has already committed adultery with her in his heart. (Matthew 5:27-28)

You can see how Jesus is separating the letter from the spirit of the law by the way that He phrases His words: "You have heard that it was said...But I say to you." The letter of the Law says "Do not commit adultery." The spirit of the law says "Do not have an adulterous heart." There is a big difference between these two because it is possible to never commit the act of adultery and yet still have an impure and adulterous heart. Jesus said that we should "first cleanse the inside of the cup and dish, that the outside of them may be clean also" (Matthew 23:26). Changing outward behavior does not ensure inner purity, but cleansing the inside will certainly cause a positive change of behavior. Therefore, Jesus cut to the spirit of the law.

There are plenty of other examples that we could look at, but I think this example gets the point across. It is not enough to know and teach what the Bible says. Effective teaching means that we must interpret it properly and get to the real meaning behind the words. Remember, "The letter kills, but the Spirit gives life" (2 Corinthians 3:6).

Explaining in Simple Terms

Good teachers have the ability to take complex concepts and explain them in a simple way so that even new believers and the unlearned can understand. Teachers are explainers. The job of a teacher is not to impress people with how smart they are or how much they know. It is to break down the teachings of the Word into ways that even a child can understand.

This does not mean that we water down the message or that we cannot delve into deep truths of the Word. It is possible to speak with depth and even get into the Greek and Hebrew meaning of words and still teach in such a way that people can understand you. The teachings of the Bible are not meant for an intellectually elite class of people. Jesus was able to relate to the common people—this is one of the traits of an effective teacher.

Teaching the Whole Counsel of God

And finally, effective teaching instructs people in the whole counsel of God. It is important that people are grounded in the fullness of truth and not just certain individual doctrines of God's Word. There are certain things that the Bible teaches that seem to contradict each other apart from seeing the big picture and being grounded in the whole counsel of God. Overemphasizing one doctrine over another will cause the people of God to be lopsided in their thinking and living. There is a tremendous need for true balance in our teaching.

God is a multi-faceted being with a multi-faceted nature. He is holy and just as well as merciful and loving. He is good and kind but can also be fierce and stern. He is an all-compassionate Father as well as an all-consuming fire. We are called both to love God and fear God and to be both His servants and His friends. Jesus is both the Lion of the tribe of Judah and the gentle Lamb of God. The amazing thing is that all of these things are true at the same time. We need to teach the whole picture of who God is and not just part of His character.

This type of balance in teaching applies to many other areas as well. We need to teach a balance of the sovereignty of God and the responsibility of man; between the fruit of the Spirit and the gifts of the Spirit; between humility and boldness; between the Word of God and the Spirit of God; between God's mercy and grace and His judgment and power. Like Paul told the church in Ephesus, we need to be able to say "I have not shunned to declare to you the whole counsel of God" (Acts 20:27).

Having Ears to Hear

When Jesus rose from the dead, He explained to the disciples that His death on the cross was a fulfillment of what was written in the Law and Prophets. Then it says that "He opened their minds to understand the Scriptures" (Luke 24:45 ESV). The Word of God is designed to be understood through the illumination of the Holy Spirit. It is not like a textbook that is primarily comprehended through academic study. Therefore, when we read the Bible or listen to teaching, we should ask the Holy Spirit to open our hearts and minds to truly receive what He is trying to teach us.

One of the common ways that Jesus taught was through parables. Matthew 13:3 says, "Then He spoke many things to them in parables." Parables are fictional stories that contain spiritual truth. They are like riddles that need to be solved. Parables employ the use of symbolism, often using everyday items to symbolize spiritual things. For example, in the Parable of the Sower found Matthew, Mark, and Luke, Jesus used the illustration of a farmer sowing seed into different types of soil to represent how the Word of God is sown into the hearts of mankind.

The nature of the parables that Jesus used were such that only those with ears to hear would be able to understand their true meaning. He often ended His parables with the statement "he who has ears to hear, let him hear!" (Matthew 11:15). It is not that they were complicated or intellectually advanced, but that they needed to be perceived through spiritual revelation by those who were hungry.

The beautiful thing about parables is that once we get a revelation as to what they mean, we have gained an understanding of how things look in the eyes of God. Using the example of the Parable of the Sower again, we see that God views His Word as a seed to be planted in the hearts of people in order to produce the fruit He desires. In the Parable of the Unmerciful Servant found in Matthew 18:21-35, we see God's perspective on forgiveness. He sees our sin as a debt that could never be paid apart from the cross. Other people's sin against us is seen as a much smaller debt in comparison to what our sin was against God. The Parable of the Lost Sheep, the Lost Coin, and the Prodigal Son in Luke 15 gives us insight into the heart of God for the lost.

Because of the symbolism and oftentimes hidden meaning of His parables, the disciples would ask Jesus to explain the meaning of the parables to them. This is a good picture of one of the purposes of parables and teaching in general for that matter. They should draw us to Jesus to seek Him for an answer. Those who were content to remain on the outside would not get the benefit of the further revelation, but those who were hungry enough to press in would.

> And the disciples came and said to Him, "Why do You speak to them in parables?" He answered and said to them, "Because it has been given to you to know the mysteries of the kingdom of heaven, but to them it has not been given. For whoever has, to him more will be given, and he will have abundance; but whoever does not have, even what he has will be taken away from him. Therefore I speak to them in parables, because seeing they do not see, and hearing they do not hear, nor do they understand. (Matthew 13:10-13)

Jesus' use of parables ensured that only the hungry and sincere seeker would be able to understand them. Your level of hunger will often determine your level of revelation. When you are hungry for the Word of God, He will reveal things to you that the satisfied will not see. Then Jesus will say of you, "Blessed are your eyes for they see, and your ears for they hear" (Matthew 13:16).

Knowing the Teacher

In the days of Jesus, the Pharisees were able to quote Scripture and teach it to others. They knew God's written Word better than anybody around. But when the living Word came to earth, they did not recognize Him. Jesus rebuked the Pharisees for knowing the Scriptures so well but refusing to come to Him and receive true life (see John 5:38-40).

More important than being a good teacher and being trained in understanding Bible doctrine is to know the Teacher Himself. Like the Pharisees, it is actually possible to make an idol out of Bible knowledge. We must uphold the authority of Scripture, value the Bible, and treasure the Word. But we must also remember that we do not worship a Book, we worship its Author. In our teaching, let us remember to draw people to Jesus and not just to doctrines; to the Truth and not just to truths. The best outcome of our teaching is for believers to be grounded in the Word of God and walking intimately with Jesus.

5

Healing the Sick

"Jesus Christ is the same yesterday, today, and forever" (Hebrews 13:8). He is still healing the sick and setting the captives free. God is awakening the church to its spiritual inheritance in Christ, and His ministry is being restored. Below is the powerful testimony of how God healed a friend of mine of three "incurable" diseases:

> I'll never forget when I came to a collision with Truth. I met a man in a bright yellow shirt who told me that Jesus could heal me. He said it with such certainty that I wondered if he was talking about my properly stuffed-in-a-box-of-religion Jesus or if perhaps he knew something I didn't. It was worth finding out.

It had taken years for the doctors to give three names to my condition: Lupus, Fibromyalgia, and Hypoglycemia. While my immune system was at war with itself and my legs frequently gave way to a wheel chair, my heart was slowly giving in to a life of grief, sorrow, pain, sickness, anger, and despair. Until I met Him. The week following my odd encounter with this man, I began my frantic search through the Scriptures. God, being totally awesome in His exact timing, had me house-sitting for my only Christian friend whose house was laden with Bibles and books on God's healing ways.

It was Isaiah 53:4-5 that especially broke through to my heart, and I thought, *if Jesus already paid the price, then I am healed, and there's no reason to hurt like this.* And I believed exactly what the Scripture said. I then began to speak the healing Scriptures over myself (especially Isaiah 53) as I forced myself to literally take steps and walk in pain. I did this day after day until all the symptoms and pain vanished; and then I shouted to the world what He had done! This included the judge who had been ready to award me disability for the rest of my life, my lawyer who could hardly recognize me after my healing, and my doctor who confessed with his own mouth that it must have been God who did it, because there was no other way. This he said as he handed me my clean bill of health. All I did was take Jesus at His word, apply it to my life, and nothing has been the same ever since. I praise God that He has healed me and given me new life!

The Torch of Healing

The ministry of Jesus was not limited to proclamation and explanation; it was also full of demonstration. Healing the sick was a major emphasis of Christ's ministry and as said before, was one of the four major things that He did on a regular basis. Jesus walked the earth carrying a "torch" of healing so that everywhere He went the sick were healed. He cured the sick, restored the brokenhearted, and delivered the captive. This became so well known that those in need of healing would come to Him from all the surrounding regions to wherever He was ministering.

Not only did Jesus heal, but He commissioned others to do the same. He passed on the torch of healing to the twelve apostles, then to the seventy who were sent out in Luke 10, and then to the whole church (see Mark 16:15-18). The early church carried on Christ's ministry of healing as outlined in the book of Acts, but somewhere along the way we dropped the torch. Every once in a while, some saint of God comes along and picks it up, demonstrating the gospel of Christ with miracles and signs. Some of these torch carriers include John G. Lake, Smith Wigglesworth, and Kathryn Kuhlman. These are the Joshuas and Calebs who ventured into the promised land and brought back of its fruit for the body of Christ to see. We often look back on these ministers with awe, never realizing that we too are meant to enter in, pick up the torch of healing, and carry on the ministry of Christ.

The Importance of Healing

"Lord, have mercy on my son, for he is an epileptic and suffers severely; for he often falls into the fire and often into the water. So I brought him to Your disciples, but they could not cure him." Then Jesus answered and said, "O faithless and perverse generation, how long shall I be with you? How long shall I bear with you? Bring him here to Me." (Matthew 17:15-17)

What would cause Jesus to get so agitated as to call His generation faithless and perverse? Murder? Homosexuality? Rebellion? Actually, it was the inability of His disciples to heal an epileptic boy. Healing was so normal in the ministry of Jesus that it was totally shocking to see someone not get healed. His heart must break over the inability of His disciples to heal today. Not only is there a general powerlessness to heal the sick, many churches do not even attempt to pray for the sick and some actually oppose and speak against those who do. We need to wake up and begin to contend for the ministry of healing to be completely restored in our day!

To neglect or oppose the ministry of healing is to neglect or oppose one of the things that Jesus did most. In light of Christ's example of healing, the believers' commission to heal, and the commands of Scripture to pray for the sick, one would think that healing would be a natural part of the Christian life. As it is, with some exceptions, the ministry of healing is being neglected by Jesus' modern-day disciples.

Healing was important to Jesus for many reasons. It showed the compassion of God, demonstrated the power of the gospel, and testified to who He was. It manifested the kingdom of God on earth, showed the devil's defeat, and brought people to Himself. The early church also saw healing as an important element of ministry and the miraculous would sometimes be the catalyst for whole cities turning to God (see Acts 9:32-35).

The above Matthew 17 passage shows just how important healing was to Jesus. He would not leave the boy in his tormented state but cast out the spirit and set him free from his sickness. Healing was not some side issue or something that Jesus was neutral about. After the disciples' failed attempt, it would have been easy for them to conclude that it must not have been God's will to heal the boy but not in Jesus' eyes. The problem was not with God but with the disciples.

My Journey into Healing

Praying for the sick was not normal in the church that I grew up in. In fact, I can't remember one instance of ever seeing it happen. So even after I had begun seriously seeking the Lord and was baptized in the Holy Spirit, I was a little skeptical about any claims of healing that I would hear. I thought that if healings were happening today, surely it would be on the news or on the front page of the newspaper. I was warned to be careful about those "crazy faith healers." But studying the subject of prayer led me to the subject of the Holy Spirit. The subject of the Holy Spirit led me to learn about spiritual gifts, and this led me to learn about healing.

Once I was convinced about what the Bible said about healing and learned that there were reputable people who were experiencing genuine healings today, it was over. I bought some anointing oil and began to pray for the sick. Everywhere I went I carried the oil in my pocket and looked for opportunities to pray for anyone who needed healing. I was determined to pray out of obedience to God regardless of whether or not anyone got healed. And at first, nobody did.

I will never forget the first time someone was healed through my prayers. I was a senior in college and was leading a Christian athlete Bible study that met every Thursday night. One night a guy on my leadership team came to the Bible study on crutches. He was a wrestler and had chipped a bone in his shin. After the Bible study was over, he asked me if I would pray for his shin and I agreed. I anointed him with oil, prayed for him, and then went home. I didn't feel a thing while praying, and as far as I could tell nothing had happened. About twenty minutes later he called to tell me that his shin was completely healed. He had walked all the way home without his crutches and all the pain was gone. I could hardly believe it!

Since that first miracle I have seen many other healings take place, but there are still many times when nothing tangible happens after prayer. The only proper response is to continue to stand upon the truth of God's Word and minister to the sick in faith so that further breakthrough can be achieved.

Keys for Healing Ministry

If we are going to pick up and carry the torch of healing the sick, it is vital that we have a renewing of the mind as to how we view sickness and the ministry of healing. Through the study of Scripture, practical experience, and learning from those with powerful healing ministries both past and present, I have found the following four keys to be essential to a mindset of faith for healing.

1. It is God's Will to Heal

One time a leper came to Jesus begging to be healed and saying, "If you are willing you can make me clean." He did not question His *ability* to heal but His *willingness* to heal. Many struggle with the same question today. Jesus said to the leper, "I am willing" and then He healed him (see Mark 1:40-41). As we read through the gospels, we see that Jesus was always willing to heal the sick.

In order to have faith to minister healing to the sick, we must be absolutely convinced from the Scriptures that it is God's will to heal. Faith cannot exist where there is no certainty about God's will. Healing must become a conviction that is based on the Bible alone and not on experience. Jesus always did the will of God and Jesus was always healing people. There is not one instance recorded in Scripture of someone asking for healing and Jesus turning them down.

When I talk to people about healing being the will of God there is always a question that arises: "What about so-and-so who did not get healed?" Everybody knows of somebody who has died of a sickness. In some cases, the sick person believed God for healing and had been prayed for many times, with other people interceding and fasting for their healing.

So, if it is God's will to heal, why doesn't everybody get healed? The best way I know how to answer that question is with the following statement: *God's will does not automatically happen on earth.* That is why Jesus instructed us to pray for His will to be done on earth like it is in heaven (see Matthew 6:10). Just because a person did not get healed does not mean it was not God's will to heal them. There are various factors involved and certainly an element of mystery to be embraced. But God's desire to heal is seen throughout the Bible. When healing doesn't come, we must not automatically assume it was not God's will.

There are some instances in the Bible where sickness comes upon people because of judgment (see 2 Kings 5:26-27, Acts 13:6-12, and Revelation 2:20-23 for a few examples). While this is the case, it doesn't negate the truth that it is generally God's desire to heal. (In the same way, it is God's will for all to be saved and yet many are not.) We have to remember that we are not yet walking in the fullness of the promises of God. Instead of lowering the standard of Scripture, we need to contend for our promised land and see more and more people healed.

2. Sickness is of the Devil

When you read the accounts of healing in the gospels, it becomes evident that Jesus saw sickness as an enemy to be destroyed. He saw sickness as a work of the devil. "And behold, there was a woman who had a spirit of infirmity eighteen years, and was bent over and could in no way raise herself up" (Luke 13:11). Here we have a woman who had a back condition that today we might call scoliosis. Notice the source of the sickness: a spirit of infirmity. Jesus ministered healing to her, and since it was a Sabbath day, the Pharisees found fault with Him. Look at Jesus' response in verse 16:

"So ought not this woman, being a daughter of Abraham, whom *Satan has bound*—think of it—for eighteen years, be loosed from this bond on the Sabbath?" (emphasis added). Jesus said that her infirmity was a bondage caused by Satan.

Acts 10:38 says that "God anointed Jesus of Nazareth with the Holy Spirit and with power, who went about doing good and healing all who were oppressed by the devil, for God was with Him." We are to view sickness as Jesus did; a work of Satan that needs to be destroyed. It is something that is to be fought against and not put up with or embraced.

Like the story from Luke 13 above, there are other examples from Christ's ministry where the source of sickness was an evil spirit. We see this in the case of an epileptic boy and a man who is mute (see Matthew 17:14-21; Matthew 9:32-33). This is also true of Paul's ministry: "Now God worked unusual miracles by the hands of Paul, so that even handkerchiefs or aprons were brought from his body to the sick, and the diseases left them and the evil spirits went out of them" (Acts 19:11-12). It says that the handkerchiefs were brought to the *sick* and as a result the diseases left them *and the evil spirits went out of them*. It is clear from Scripture that demons can cause sickness.

Understanding that sickness is a work of the devil in a general sense gives me a greater passion to see the sick healed, and knowing that specific diseases can be caused by evil spirits affects the way that I pray for healing. I have seen people physically healed while going through deliverance prayer without even praying specifically for the area of needed healing. One example is a student of mine when I was teaching at a Christian school who was having pain in her neck. I prayed for her to be healed and there was no positive result. The next week she became aware of a possible need to be delivered from evil spirits. When another teacher and I led her through prayer and deliverance, she was set free from several demonic spirits in a visible way. After the time of prayer her neck was completely healed even though we never addressed it in the prayer time.

Not every sickness is caused by an evil spirit. But sickness is a result of the fall of man and is a work of the devil.

3. Healing is in the Atonement

There are several times in the Bible where the healing of sickness and the forgiveness of sin are tied together. For instance, Psalm 103:2-3 says, "Bless the Lord, O my soul, and forget not all His benefits: Who forgives all your iniquities, who heals all your diseases." Jesus' death on the cross not only paid the price for sin to be forgiven but also for sickness to be healed. This teaching is commonly called *healing in the atonement*. Though contested by some well-known Bible teachers, it is taught by Scripture.

Matthew 8:16-17 says, "When evening had come, they brought to Him many who were demon-possessed. And He cast out the spirits with a word, and healed all who were sick, that it might be fulfilled which was spoken by Isaiah the prophet, saying:

"He Himself took our infirmities
And bore our sicknesses."

Matthew is quoting from Isaiah 53, the famous foreshadowing of the Messiah's suffering. This is the same passage that says,

"But He was wounded for our transgressions,
He was bruised for our iniquities;
The chastisement for our peace was upon Him,
And by His stripes we are healed." (Verse 5)

On the same cross Jesus bore our sins and our sicknesses. The fact that Matthew connected Isaiah 53 to the physical healings that Jesus was performing leaves no room to spiritualize Isaiah's use of the word healed in verse five. It means exactly what it says. "By His stripes we are *healed*." Jesus has paid the price for healing. So, let's contend for healing to be restored so that He gets the fullness of what He paid for.

4. Jesus Healed as a Man

When I first realized the truth that Jesus did His entire ministry, including His miracles, as a man, it was a paradigm shift for me. Jesus is God, and I had always assumed that this is what enabled Him to heal. But this is not what the Bible teaches. Jesus humbled Himself to become a man and chose not to use His power as God (see Philippians 2:5-11). This truth is important to understand, because if Jesus was able to heal and perform other miracles only because He was God, we could never be expected to follow in His footsteps. But if He did it as a man, He paved the way for us to do it as well.

I know that this teaching can make some people nervous or to claim that we are denying the divinity of Christ. But this is not the case at all. The Bible teaches that Jesus is fully God and fully man. We must not deny His divinity or His humanity. To deny His humanity is just as much a distortion of His nature as to deny His divinity. Jesus is God, but He did not function in ministry as God. He chose to function as a man. This is why He could be tempted. This is why He could be tired. This is why He constantly prayed. This is why He relied on the leading and power of the Holy Spirit. He did not even begin His ministry until being anointed with the Holy Spirit and then tested in the wilderness for forty days.

One time when the Pharisees accused Jesus of using the devil's power to cast out demons, He said, "But if I cast out demons *by the Spirit of God*, surely the kingdom of God has come upon you" (Matthew 12:28, emphasis added). Acts 10:38, a passage that was quoted earlier in this chapter, shows that Jesus healed, because He was anointed with power and because the Father was with Him. These and other passages make it plain that Jesus was able to heal not because He was God but because He was empowered by the Holy Spirit—the same Holy Spirit who lives in us.

Jesus' Model of Healing

As we pick up the torch of healing and pursue the ministry of Jesus, we will face many obstacles and much opposition. It will take perseverance and an attitude of steadfast faith in order to see this ministry restored. There will be many opportunities to give up the fight; it truly is a battle to take possession of our spiritual inheritance. Keeping the above principles in mind will help us to persevere when the times get tough, and studying the example of Christ will give us more understanding for how to heal the sick. Because He was so Spirit-led, I hesitate to even use the word model when describing Christ's ministry of healing. But there are some principles that we can learn and apply as we seek to follow in His footsteps, take the torch of healing, and begin to heal the sick.

We often use the term praying for the sick, but technically speaking this is not accurate. Jesus did not pray for the sick; He healed the sick. You cannot find one instance in the gospels where Jesus asked the Father to heal somebody. Instead, you will see Him making authoritative commands and pronouncements of healing or simply placing His hands on the person to heal them. He healed a leper by speaking the words "be cleansed." He healed a paralytic by commanding him to "rise up and walk." He raised a young girl from the dead with the command "little girl, arise." Sometimes He healed a person by casting a demon out of them. Sometimes He used unorthodox methods like putting mud on a blind man's eyes. Not once do we see Him petitioning God to heal.

When you survey the healing ministry of the early disciples, you will find very similar methods being used. Peter spoke to the paralyzed man at the temple and commanded him to "rise and walk," and he once raised a woman from the dead with the command "Tabitha, arise." Paul also healed a paralyzed man with a similar command and sometimes used unusual methods such as taking handkerchiefs to sick people. The early church healed the sick the same way that Jesus did.

We know that no human being has the power to heal anybody; Jesus is the Healer. However, we are so intimately involved in the process that the Bible actually says that we are to heal the sick. In Matthew 10:8 Jesus commissioned the twelve apostles, telling them to "heal the sick, cleanse the lepers, raise the dead, cast out demons." Mark 6:13 says, "And they cast out many demons, and anointed with oil many who were sick, and healed them." We need to move beyond praying for the sick and into healing the sick.

Whenever I am ministering to a person in need of healing, I will generally do two things. First, I will welcome the presence and power of the Holy Spirit. Then, I will make authoritative commands based on the specific situation. I was the guest speaker at a retreat once and on the final night I had a word of knowledge that somebody needed healing in the hip area. During the prayer ministry time, a young lady came up to me and told me that she had a problem with her hips; they were unevenly aligned and this was causing her to have pain in her back and giving her other problems. She sat down in a chair, and my wife laid hands on her hips. I then welcomed the Holy Spirit and began to command her hips to come into proper alignment. As soon as I gave the command, her whole body jolted, her hips lifted off the chair, and then shifted into place. Just like that she was healed.

It is not that we should never use the word pray when referring to ministering to the sick; it is just that we need to make commands instead of petitions. When we make authoritative commands for healing we need to realize a few things. First, we are not commanding God. In Mark 11:23 Jesus said, "For assuredly, I say to you, whoever says to this mountain, 'Be removed and be cast into the sea,' and does not doubt in his heart, but believes that those things he says will be done, he will have whatever he says." Jesus said that we are to speak to the mountain—the specific problem or situation—and command it to move, but we are never to command God Himself. Secondly, this authority is not of ourselves but belongs to Jesus Christ and must be done in His name. This type of authority comes from being in Christ and having total faith in His Word.

The more anointing and authority we walk in the simpler the ministry of healing will become. As we take back more and more ground in this area, we will spend less time praying and interceding and more time healing and commanding things into God's order. After all, Jesus has already paid the price for the healing of mankind. I long for the day when we have meetings in which every sick person gets healed. "And great multitudes followed Him, and He healed them all" (Matthew 12:15).

In the next chapter we will discuss a ministry that is closely related to the ministry of healing and that is the ministry of deliverance.

6

Deliverance from Demons

"In the name of Jesus, I command the spirit of oppression to come out," I said while leading the congregation in a prayer for deliverance. A young lady who had been battling dark depression and tormenting suicidal thoughts felt something lift off and leave her. After years of struggle, she was instantly set free from depression and suicide.

Another time while leading a corporate prayer for deliverance I said, "I command the fear of death and the spirit of death to come out!" A woman in the congregation instantly bent over, not able to raise herself up, and was delivered that night. She had been struggling with an increasing irrational fear of her husband dying. Every day she thought would be his last day, and she was even planning for his funeral. But from that moment on, she was set free and at peace in her mind.

A young man had been through a traumatic childhood in the foster care system. He struggled with rejection, pornography, and same-sex attraction. He ended up coming to one of my deliverance meetings, not even sure if he really believed in deliverance. But God met him during the ministry time and he was radically set free from trauma and bondage to sin.

I could continue to share testimony after testimony of people being set free from demonic oppression, bondage, torment, and affliction. Over the past number of years, I have led thousands of people through prayers for deliverance in both large group and individual ministry settings. One thing I can tell you: the need to see the ministry of deliverance restored to the church is great!

What is deliverance, and how is it relevant for Christians today? Read on as we dive into this controversial but important aspect of the ministry of Jesus.

Removing the Grave Clothes

> Now when He had said these things, He cried with a loud voice, "Lazarus, come forth!" And he who had died came out bound hand and foot with graveclothes, and his face was wrapped with a cloth. Jesus said to them, "Loose him, and let him go." (John 11:43-44)

John 11 tells the story of Lazarus being raised from the dead. After being in the tomb for four days, the Lord rose him up with the simple words "Lazarus, come forth!" Even dead people have to obey the voice of Jesus, and so Lazarus emerged from the tomb. He was perfectly alive, but he was still bound with graveclothes, and so the next command was "Loose him, and let him go."

Many Christians today find themselves in a similar situation as Lazarus was between the two commands. They have received God's salvation and have been raised from the dead spiritually, but they are still bound by "graveclothes." They know that they are forgiven, but they have not experienced the true freedom that Christ purchased for them on the cross. They have heard the message of salvation ("Lazarus, come forth!") but not the message of deliverance ("Loose him, and let him go"). They go through life in a cycle of defeat, bound by fear, addictions, depression, wounds of the past, bitterness, sin, and a host of other graveclothes.

The saddest part about this situation is that these are sincere believers who go to church week after week. They are asked to get involved and serve in their local church, but no one seems to notice the graveclothes, and it's hard to serve when your hands and feet are tied. It's hard to move forward in your walk with the Lord and grow in a deep relationship with God when you are bound with chains of oppression. It is hard to have your mind renewed when there is demonic torment bringing intrusive thoughts and images. The truth is that God never intended salvation without deliverance. And yet many Christians are in desperate need of this vital ministry. Have you ever wondered if some of the struggles and problems you face contain a demonic element?

Deliverance refers to casting out demons which are also called unclean spirits or evil spirits throughout the New Testament. Jesus spent a considerable amount of time involved in this practice. Mark 1:39 (NASB) says, "And He went into their synagogues throughout all Galilee, preaching and casting out the demons." According to this verse it was as common for Jesus to cast out a demon as it was for Him to preach a sermon. As we have seen, it was one of the four major ministries that He did in His earthly ministry. This was not some every-once-in-a while event; it was normal, everyday ministry. In a modern equivalent this verse might say, "And Jesus traveled throughout the United States. He went from church to church preaching and driving demons out of people." Yes, if Jesus were on the earth ministering today in the United States (or anywhere else) that is exactly what He would be doing.

As stated in the introduction of this book, when I gave my life to the Lord, I experienced a tremendous amount of freedom from specific bondages to sin. At first, I just assumed that this freedom was what every Christian was experiencing. But it didn't take long for me to realize that many Christians are not experiencing the freedom that Christ has promised us. Many are still wrapped in the graveclothes of sin, torment, and other bondages. As I realized this, the topic of freedom in Christ became a passion of mine, and I began to have an intense desire to see other people experience the freedom that the Lord had given to me. However, I did not have an understanding of how the ministry of deliverance was related to this.

Calling into Deliverance

During my junior year in college, I had a conversation with a good friend of mine about the topic of deliverance from demons. I was wondering why Jesus had cast out demons so regularly in His ministry, and yet I had never seen one instance of this happening in all my years of attending church. This didn't seem to add up to me and I knew that we were missing something, but I wasn't sure what I was supposed to do about it.

That night the Lord gave me a dream indicating that I would be involved in the ministry of deliverance. In the dream I was at an all-you-can-eat buffet restaurant. I was hungry and left the table to get more food from the buffet. As I went, I noticed a man with a very dark appearance and an evil look in his eyes. When I sat down to eat, the man started to walk right toward my table. I stood up and felt the power of God well up within me. Immediately I perceived that the man had a demon, and with this fresh empowerment and boldness from God, I began to command the demon to come out of the man in Jesus' name. The demon left him and he rejoiced in his newfound freedom, and then I awoke.

At the time of this dream, I didn't really understand its meaning but was certain that it was from the Lord. I actually thought I was going to run into the man I had seen in the dream and was going to have to cast a demon out of him—which was a very scary prospect to me! I later realized that the dream was symbolic. The all-you-can-eat buffet represented the teaching of God's Word and as I continued to feed on it, He would give me spiritual discernment to recognize the presence of demons and empower me to cast them out. In the coming months and years, this is exactly what happened.

Soon after this dream, I began to have other dreams of a similar nature where I would find myself casting evil spirits out of people. I wasn't sure what to make of it all, except that I felt like God was going to call me to be involved in deliverance. During this time, I came across some books with teaching on deliverance. My mind was renewed with biblical clarity and I began to see the world through a new lens. I began to step out and pray for people who needed deliverance, see demons cast out, and watch the chains of demonic influence be removed from their lives.

Myths and Misunderstandings

The devil works through ignorance and fear. I believe that in the Western culture the primary weapon of the enemy to keep people from deliverance is ignorance. Generally speaking, there is widespread unawareness of the whole topic of the spiritual realm and the need to free people from evil spirits today. We tend to intellectualize everything and explain things in strictly natural terms. This leads to skepticism over any talk of spirit-beings or supernatural encounters. As a result of this ignorance, many of God's people are suffering unnecessarily; perishing for lack of knowledge (see Hosea 4:6).

In other "less sophisticated" areas of the world where they are not so ignorant of the spiritual realm, many people are dominated by a fear of demons. In this type of setting, superstition flourishes and much effort is spent on trying to appease spirits through charms, sacrifices, or other rituals. This equates to the worship of demons and is a terrible bondage. But whether it is ignorance, fear, or a combination of the two, something is keeping us from fulfilling this ministry that was obviously very important to Jesus.

There are many myths and misunderstandings that surround the whole subject of deliverance ministry. These misunderstandings cause us to have a skewed view of what this ministry is about and how important and relevant it actually is for us today. Before I came to an understanding of casting out demons I held to these myths, and I have found that they are commonly held views in much of the church.

Myth 1: Deliverance from evil spirits is a very rare need.

Many believers who would never deny the existence of the spirit world and the fact that demons can inhabit people assume that it is extremely rare to come across a person needing deliverance. Often this ministry is relegated to the mission field in faraway third-world countries. The problem with this thinking is that it does not line up with the ministry of Jesus.

It was not a rare thing for Jesus to cast out a demon. In fact, according to Mark 1:39 which was quoted earlier, it would have been rarer for Jesus to go somewhere and *not* cast out demons. This verse also states that the casting out of demons was happening in the synagogues which would be equivalent to our churches. This teaches us that ordinary church-going people, and not just the far-out ones like the man with the legion in Mark 5:1-20, can need to be delivered from evil spirits.

Not only did Jesus cast out demons on a regular basis, He also commissioned His followers to do the same. In fact, He never sent out His disciples to preach without first giving them authority to drive out demons. This was true of the twelve, then of the seventy in Luke 10, and finally of all believers in Mark 16:17 which says, "And these signs will follow those who believe: In My name they will cast out demons." Deliverance was obviously a common need in that time and nothing has changed today. While there are varying degrees of demonic influence, it is not rare for a person to need deliverance.

Myth 2: It is always obvious when a person has a demon.

I used to think that if a person had a demon, it would be blatantly obvious to everyone. When I was in college there was a homeless man who would walk the streets yelling curse words and other random things at people with a wild look in his eyes. He was known as "Crazy Mike," and he was the type of person who I assumed could *possibly* have a demon.

The truth is, when a person has an evil spirit it is not usually obvious. Demons prefer to dwell in darkness, not wanting their presence to be exposed by the light. Once when Jesus was teaching in a synagogue, a man with an unclean spirit began to manifest and Jesus cast the spirit out (see Mark 1:21-26). The spirit was not always outwardly manifesting in this person's life, but as Jesus taught with authority, it was exposed to the light and forced out.

Several years ago, I was a leader at a youth retreat where the guest speaker preached on the power of the Holy Spirit. When students came forward for prayer, one particular middle school girl fell to the ground after having hands laid on her. I noticed that as she lay on the floor, she began to act strange, and I soon realized that a demon was manifesting. I pulled her to the side, commanded the spirit to leave, and out it went. You would have never known that this young girl needed to be delivered from a demon, but the anointing of the Spirit stirred up the evil spirit and forced it into the light so that it could be cast out.

One reason for the confusion concerning deliverance ministry is the English terminology commonly used to describe people who need deliverance in the Bible: *demon-possessed*. A more accurate term based on the original Greek would be "demonized" or to "have a demon." When a person has a demon (or multiple demons), it does not mean that they are possessed which implies total ownership. Instead, each spirit affects a particular area of the person's life or personality. In line with this thought, Scripture shows that demons have specific names that correlate to their functions. For example, in Luke 13:11 we see a woman who was bent over because of a spirit of infirmity. The Bible also describes a spirit of fear, a spirit of heaviness, and many other examples.

Myth 3: A Christian cannot have a demon.

This is perhaps the most commonly held and most damaging myth concerning the ministry of deliverance. There are many, even among those who believe in the gifts of the Spirit and ministry of healing, who hold to this view. It is primarily based on the following premise: Christians are the temple of the Holy Spirit, and an evil spirit cannot dwell in the same place as the Spirit of God. This seems to be a good argument but really has no scriptural foundation. It is based more on human logic than biblical truth. Using this same logic, you would also have to conclude that it is impossible for a believer to sin or ever have an evil thought. For how can sin — which is contrary to God's nature — be in His temple? How can evil thoughts be in the mind of a believer when we have the mind of Christ (see 1 Corinthians 2:16)? Yet, we know that believers do stumble into sin and that they can and do have evil thoughts at times. The same people who argue that a Christian cannot have a demon would never argue that it is impossible for a Christian to sin or have a dark thought. This is inconsistent logic.

Just like idols were brought into the Old Testament temple, evil spirits can gain entrance into the New Testament temple (our bodies) if there are open doors. Just like the manifest presence of God dwelt in the Holy of Holies in the temple, the Holy Spirit dwells in the human spirit of a believer. I do not believe that an evil spirit can enter into a believer's spirit but certainly can dwell in the body or soul.

Consider 2 Corinthians 11:4 (ESV, emphasis added): "For if someone comes and proclaims another Jesus than the one we proclaimed, or if you *receive a different spirit* from the one you received, or if you accept a different gospel from the one you accepted, you put up with it readily enough." Paul warned the Corinthian believers that if they received a different gospel or a different Jesus, they could also receive a different spirit than the Holy Spirit. This should be evidence enough that it is possible for a Christian to have a demon. There is nothing in Scripture that says that all demons automatically leave a person when they are saved or that a saved person is automatically precluded from having evil spirits.

In Matthew 15:26 Jesus referred to deliverance ministry as "the children's bread" meaning that it belongs to the children of God. Holding to a belief system that says that a Christian cannot have a demon deprives the children of their bread, leaving countless Christians bound in "graveclothes" with no hope of freedom in sight. I have seen countless solid believers set free from demons that had a grip on certain areas of their lives.

Myth 4: We don't need to worry about demons. Focus on Jesus.

The fourth and final myth that I want to deal with states that talking about demons and deliverance ministry gives too much attention to the devil and that we should just focus all of our attention on Jesus. I wish it were that easy. It is definitely possible to be over-fascinated with the realm of darkness and become more focused on deliverance ministry than necessary, and I too would caution against this. However, ignoring the devil does not make him go away. In fact, Paul specifically says that we should not be ignorant of his schemes and that we should take an active stand against him (see 2 Corinthians 2:11 and Ephesians 6:10-12).

If we ignore the ministry of casting out demons, we have just removed a major portion of the ministry of Christ. While deliverance ministry should not be seen as an end in itself, it is often a critical step in a person gaining true freedom and fulfilling their destiny in God.

We need to follow the example of Jesus. He was not obsessed with demons; He confronted them for the purpose of setting people free. He was not looking for some spiritual power trip or trying to cause a spectacle but was moved with the Father's compassion to set captives free. Some in the deliverance movement have taken things to unbiblical extremes or have used bizarre methods causing others to shy away from the ministry as a whole. But the presence of extremes and distortions does not give us the right to ignore the example and commands of Christ. He has called us to follow His example in casting out demons to set captives free!

Open Doors

One of the keys to understanding the ministry of deliverance is the revelation that to the spirit world, the human body is a house. God sees the human body as a potential dwelling place. Scripture calls the body of the believer the temple of the Holy Spirit (see 1 Corinthians 6:19). But the devil and his demons also see the human body as a place to live.

When an unclean spirit goes out of a man, he goes through dry places, seeking rest, and finds none. Then he says, 'I will return to my house from which I came.' And when he comes, he finds it empty, swept, and put in order. Then he goes and takes with him seven other spirits more wicked than himself, and they enter and dwell there; and the last state of that man is worse than the first." (Matthew 12:43-45)

Notice that the unclean spirit in this passage referred to the man as his house. Evil spirits crave bodies to live in and to express their nature through. Without such a body they are restless, just like a homeless person. But a demon cannot simply enter into any person that they choose; there must be an open door in the house for it to have entrance. There are several things that can open the door for demonic access into people's lives, whether or not they are believers. These open doors give evil spirits a place to enter and dwell in the person. While not exhaustive, below is a list that briefly describes some of these openings.

Ongoing Sin

When we fail to confess and repent of sin, we come into agreement with the devil, and this gives him a right to an area of our lives. Blatant rebellious sin or ongoing hidden sin can be a demonic entry point. I believe that it was the ongoing greed and theft in Judas' life that allowed Satan to enter him. Paul warns that if we don't properly deal with anger, it can give place to the devil (see Ephesians 4:26-27). When a person cannot gain freedom from a sinful habit, there is the possibility of a demonic spirit that needs to be cast out. If it is simply the flesh, it must be crucified. But if it is a demon, it must be driven out.

Traumatic Experiences

When a person goes through a traumatic experience, sometimes a demon can gain access. Being sinned against or exploited can open the door. For example, being abused sexually, physically, or verbally can give spirits entry into the person and cause them to be bound by that traumatic experience. It seems unfair that a person can become demonized through another person's action, but the devil does not play fair. Various types of traumatic events, and all types of abuse, can open the door to demonic oppression.

Believing the Enemy's Lies

The devil is called the father of lies, and when we believe his lies we come into agreement with him. I have prayed for people who had become demonized by believing the lie that they had committed the unpardonable sin. When we believe a lie about God or about ourselves, we open the way for a lying spirit to reinforce that lie in our lives.

Exposure to Unholy Things

Being exposed to unholy things can open the door to demons. Some examples would include pornography, horror movies, and dark music. There is a reason why God commands His people to come out from among the world and be holy.

Withholding Forgiveness

Having bitterness, resentment, or unforgiveness toward others is an open door for evil spirits. I encourage you to read the parable of the unmerciful servant found in Matthew 18:15-35. At the end of the parable the unforgiving servant is put into a prison to be tormented. Withholding forgiveness from others puts you into a spiritual prison and gives the devil permission to torment you; this is a serious issue and a major root cause for many other problems. We must learn to forgive the ones who have hurt us and walk through the process of releasing them to the Lord. This does not mean that what they did was okay, and it does not mean that you cannot maintain boundaries with those who hurt you. But we must choose to walk in forgiveness as God has forgiven us.

Involvement in False Religion, Cults, and False Teaching

Behind every idol is a demon (see 1 Corinthians 10:19-20) and false teaching carries with it a false spirit (see 2 Corinthians 11:4 and 1 Timothy 4:1). It makes sense therefore, that those who become involved with cults and who believe false teachings can become demonized. Whether it is blatant false teaching like Buddhism or subtle erroneous teachings within the church, a door may be opened for a spirit to enter.

Any Occult Involvement

Contact with the occult is a major open door to the demonic and is strictly forbidden in Scripture (see Deuteronomy 18:9-12). There are two sources of supernatural power in the world: God and Satan. The word occult means "secret or hidden" and refers to the supernatural realm of Satan. Some examples include witchcraft, fortunetelling, communication with the dead, magic arts, eastern meditation, sorcery, Ouija board, astrology, Satanism, new age teachings, psychics, astral projection, and channeling. This is not an all-inclusive list but should give you an idea of what to avoid. If you have had any contact with the occult—even if it was a long time ago and it was just for fun—I encourage you to verbally renounce your involvement and seek deliverance ministry.

Curses

The last open door we will look at is the area of curses. In the West we tend to think that the idea of curses is a superstitious belief, but it is found in the Bible quite a bit. What is referred to as generational curses could certainly be an open door. This is when either sinful actions or negative attributes get passed down through a generational line. Another type of curse is what is called a word curse. James 3:8-10 talks about the tongue and how blessing and cursing can proceed from the same mouth, and Proverbs 18:21 says that death and life are in the power of the tongue. Some parents don't realize that they are literally cursing their children by saying things like "you are so stupid" or "you will never amount to anything." I have been amazed at the dramatic results when words like this were broken off of a person during a time of prayer for deliverance.

The above open doors are not necessarily a comprehensive list and much more could be said about each of them. The point is this: many times doors are opened in people's lives without them necessarily knowing it. When casting out demons, it is important to get to the root causes of the problem and make sure that every door gets closed.

How to Cast out Demons

Deliverance ministry can happen in multiple ways or settings. Sometimes there is what is referred to as a power encounter; a spontaneous clash between the Holy Spirit and evil spirits. In this scenario the anointing of the Holy Spirit stirs up demons and causes them to manifest in a person during preaching or a time of worship or prayer. The example of the youth retreat that I mentioned earlier and Jesus' encounter in the synagogue are examples of this. Another way that deliverance happens is in a private prayer ministry setting where the person comes to a location specifically to receive ministry for deliverance in a private setting. I also often minister to large groups at one time in deliverance services, churches, conferences, or other gatherings.

One of the keys for casting out demons is to discern their presence. This may come through the supernatural gift of discerning of spirits which is one of the nine manifestation gifts of the Spirit mentioned in 1 Corinthians 12. It could also come through a demonic manifestation or through simply asking a person questions and getting feedback. The more experience a person has in deliverance ministry, the more discernment they will have to recognize the presence of demons.

Once a spirit begins to manifest or has been discerned, it must be cast out. If there are any doors that need to be closed, lead the person in prayer to close each door. For example, lead them to repent of sin, forgive those who hurt them, renounce involvement in the occult, or any other relevant areas. Then, speak directly to the demon in the name of Jesus, commanding it to come out. This is what the apostle Paul did in Acts 16:18: "I command you in the name of Jesus Christ to come out of her." You do not pray for God to cast it out; you speak directly to the demon and command it to leave. We do this all in the name of Jesus, as our authority over demons come from Him and not of ourselves.

There are varying degrees of demonization and many times a person will have several demons. We can see this from the gospel accounts. Jesus cast out one demon from a man in the synagogue, seven demons out of Mary Magdalene, and probably thousands of demons out of the man with the legion. So, keep pressing in until you sense that you are at a closing point or that all the demons have left.

If a spirit is manifesting but will not leave the person, continue to command it to go in Jesus' name. But if after a while it is still not leaving, there is probably something that is giving it a right to be there and that must be dealt with. For example, the person seeking deliverance may need to forgive somebody, repent of a specific sin, or renounce involvement in the occult. If the person is not willing to do these things, then pursuing deliverance will probably not be fruitful. The person must genuinely want to be free and must be willing to meet God's conditions of breaking away from all agreement with Satan.

Demons may manifest in different ways. I have seen shaking, facial and body contortions, falling down, eyes rolled back, screaming, and many others. It is important to keep your eyes open the whole time so that you can see what is happening. Pay careful attention to the person's eyes and facial expressions. When spirits leave a person they usually leave through the mouth with some type of coughing, gagging, vomiting, shrieking, or other action of the mouth, but this does not have to happen. Sometimes there is little or no manifestation, and sometimes they leave out of places other than the mouth.

Practical Tips

There are no formulas for successful deliverance ministry and we must learn to depend on the Holy Spirit for each situation, but I hope that the information in this chapter will serve as a good foundation for those who want to begin to set captives free or those who need deliverance themselves. I want to close with just a few practical tips for deliverance ministry.

First, it is always good to minister in teams of at least two people. When Jesus sent out His disciples, He sent them two-by-two. It is good to have at least one other person present to help pray, support, and offer discernment into the situation. It is a definite wise boundary that you should never minister to a person of the opposite sex alone in a private setting. While having a team is important, it is also key that only one person be in charge of the ministry at a time or else it can get very confusing and chaotic.

Another practical tip is that we should always minister deliverance with compassion for the person receiving ministry. Don't get so caught up in confronting the demons that you forget that the person is the important one. Take time to explain to them what is happening, and in the case of longer deliverance sessions, pause frequently to ask how they are doing. Remember, the purpose is to set captives free, not get some sort of spiritual adrenaline rush.

And lastly, if possible, make sure to follow up with the person in the days and weeks that follow. Some people may need more than one prayer time to be completely set free and others need to be encouraged to do the things that will keep them free. Christians not only have to battle the devil and his demons but also the flesh and the world. Therefore, we must realize that deliverance ministry is not a cure-all or a substitute for other Christian disciplines.

We need to embrace the reality that Jesus cast out demons and that He did it on a regular basis. What would Jesus do? He would cast out demons. Obadiah 1:17 says, "But on Mount Zion there shall be deliverance, and there shall be holiness; the house of Jacob shall possess their possessions." It is time for the ministry of deliverance to be restored so that the people of God can be set free, walk in holiness, and possess the inheritance that God has for them!

....

*For more information and equipping on the topic of deliverance, check out my books *Setting Captives Free*, *Keys for Deliverance,* and *How to Minister Deliverance [Training Manual]*.

7

Authority and Power

The ministry of Jesus is being restored to the church. God wants His people to fulfill their prophetic destiny of being like Jesus and ministering like He did. He wants His church to be equipped to heal the sick and cast out demons.

Several years ago, I was on staff at a church as the youth and young adult pastor. Most of the people in our young adult ministry had never witnessed a miracle take place. I began to teach on the power of prayer and would mention the subject of healing the sick. Soon, an opportunity arose for demonstration. One of the members of the group started having pain in his chest and difficulty breathing. After seeing a doctor and getting X-rays and a CAT scan, it was determined that he had a small puncture in one of his lungs which was causing a medical condition known as Pneumothorax in which air leaks from the lung to the space around it. At the end of one of our young adult services, I suggested that we gather around him and pray for him to be healed. As we prayed, one of the other members of the group saw the Lord restoring his lung as new as a baby's. He began to breathe deeply which he was not able to do before, and the pain was instantaneously healed. Though the doctor had said it would take several weeks for his lung to heal, the Healer had other plans. That night he slept like a baby for the first time in over a week!

This was a major faith booster for our young adult ministry. We began to see other miracles of healing and deliverance take place after this first breakthrough.

Authority and Power

> Then He called His twelve disciples together and gave them power and authority over all demons, and to cure diseases. He sent them to preach the kingdom of God and to heal the sick. (Luke 9:1-2)

In order to function in the ministry of Jesus, we will need to walk in authority and power. This is what Jesus gave to His disciples when He sent them out to preach, heal, and cast out demons. Jesus Himself operated in both spiritual authority and power in each of the four facets of His own ministry that we have been examining.

What is the difference between authority and power? Authority has to do with a legal right while power has to do with divine ability. A good example that is often used to illustrate this difference is that of a police officer. His badge represents *authority*. Because of the badge, an officer has the right to pull over a speeding driver, place a criminal under arrest, and generally enforce the law. While the badge gives him a legal right, he is also equipped with various things that give him the *ability* to enforce the law. A police car, handcuffs, taser, communication system, gun, and other tools help enable him to fulfill his assignment. His badge gives him authority, and his equipment gives him power. Both are needed.

Along with a legal right, kingdom authority also has to do with having dominion over something. Jesus healed the sick, because He had dominion over sickness and disease. As we saw earlier, He never prayed to the Father for a healing but spoke directly to the circumstance at hand. He cast out demons, because He had authority over them. Let's further discuss this concept of authority as it relates to walking in the ministry of Jesus.

The Word and the Name

When Jesus was about to ascend to heaven, He spoke the following words: "All authority has been given to Me in heaven and on earth" (Matthew 28:18). After speaking these powerful words, He commissioned the disciples to go into the world and make disciples of all nations. Although all authority belongs to Jesus, He has delegated that authority to His followers who are to use that authority to advance His kingdom.

The first thing that our authority as believers is rooted in is the Word of God—we have authority because God says that we do. For example, we have authority to cast out demons, because the Word of God says so. "And these signs will follow those who believe: In My name they will cast out demons" (Mark 16:17). "Behold, I give you the authority to trample on serpents and scorpions, and over all the power of the enemy, and nothing shall by any means hurt you" (Luke 10:19). These passages declare the authority of the believer over evil spirits, giving us the right to command demons to come out of people.

God's Word has more power than anything in the universe, and all things are subject to its authority. Our authority over sin, sickness, and the devil all stem from the Word of God.

The second thing that our authority is rooted in is the name of Jesus. Notice that the Mark 16:17 passage quoted above says, "*In my name* they will cast out demons." It is not only because of the Word but because of the name of Jesus that we have the right to cast out demons. In other words, our authority is not of ourselves but in Him and from Him. Christ's name is above every other name and when we pray or speak in His name it is as if He Himself is making the petition or command. We are speaking on the basis of His finished work on the cross and the complete victory that He has won.

All of the authority that we can exercise — whether it's in preaching, teaching, healing, deliverance or otherwise — is because of the Word of God and the name of Jesus. But let us remember one thing: quoting the Word or speaking the name of Jesus is not some kind of magic formula. It needs to be in the context of a genuine relationship with God and under the leading of the Holy Spirit. God is not your personal genie, and prayer is not your way of controlling Him. The seven sons of Sceva learned a painful lesson when they tried to use the authority of Jesus' name apart from a relationship with Him. Instead of casting the demon out, they were the ones cast out naked and bleeding (see Acts 19:13-16).

Authority and Faith

Although authority is rooted in the Word of God and the name of Jesus, it must be exercised through faith. When the disciples were not able to cast a demon out of a boy, they asked Jesus why they had been unsuccessful. Consider His answer: "Because of your unbelief; for assuredly, I say to you, if you have faith as a mustard seed, you will say to this mountain, 'Move from here to there,' and it will move; and nothing will be impossible for you" (Matthew 17:20). The problem was not one of authority but of faith. One of these days we are going to believe God's Word, and mountains are going to be tossed into the sea. If we are going to speak to demons and command them to leave, we must have no doubt about our authority to do so; the same is true for sickness. Without faith the mountain isn't going anywhere.

On one occasion a centurion approached Jesus and asked Him to heal his paralyzed servant. Jesus agreed and was about to go to the centurion's house but the centurion told Jesus to only speak the word, and his servant would be healed. This centurion understood the concept of authority. He said, "For I also am a man under authority, having soldiers under me. And I say to this one, 'Go,' and he goes; and to another, 'Come,' and he comes; and to my servant, 'Do this,' and he does it" (Matthew 8:9). Jesus was astonished at the man's faith, spoke the word of healing, and the servant was healed.

Notice the centurion's line of thinking. I imagine that his thought process went something like this: *I am under the authority of my commander, and when he tells me to do something, I do it. I also have authority over soldiers, and when I speak a word, they obey. Jesus has authority over sickness so if He commands it to go, it must obey.* The centurion was right on, and his servant was healed.

Our authority is *grounded* in the Word of God and the name of Jesus, *exercised* through faith, and *released* through words. To exercise authority over demons and disease we must learn to speak to the mountain and command it to be removed. We must truly believe that God has given us authority over sin, sickness, and Satan.

The Need for Power

Not only do we need authority to operate in the ministry of Jesus, we also need supernatural power. One personal example comes to mind to illustrate this point. One evening my wife and I were praying for a young lady to receive deliverance from demons but were not making much progress. She had prayed through a prayer to close every door and take away every legal right of the enemy, and I began to command the demons to leave. The spirits were obviously being stirred up—she began to shake and felt a cold presence come over her—but they would not leave.

After about fifteen minutes of this I asked her to stand up and I asked the Holy Spirit to come and minister to her. All of the sudden she fell back under the power of God, and the demons began to come out one by one with little or no effort on my part. Supernatural discernment was given to me and the spirits were leaving faster than I could command them. Not only was she powerfully delivered, but God also completely healed her of a stomach problem that she had been suffering from for three years. Her stomach vibrated as we prayed, and God did a creative miracle!

We need power to minister as Jesus did. One of the ways this comes is through the gifts of the Holy Spirit listed in 1 Corinthians 12. These gifts are manifestations of the Spirit that can bring revelation, power, and faith. As we yield to the Holy Spirit, we can see these gifts operate through our lives in greater measure.

Jesus and the Spirit

There is no doubt that Jesus operated in supernatural power. When the woman with the issue of blood touched the hem of His garment, she felt in her body that she was healed. Jesus also felt something happen in this encounter: "But Jesus said, 'Somebody touched Me, for I perceived power going out from Me'" (Luke 8:46). There was a tangible power that had flowed from Jesus into the woman, and she was healed. Luke also mentions occasions where the power of the Lord was present to heal and where power was coming out of Jesus and healing the people (see Luke 5:17; Luke 6:19). This power that flowed through the life of Jesus was the power of the Holy Spirit. He was anointed with the Holy Spirit and power in order to do good and bring healing and freedom to those who were oppressed by the devil (see Acts 10:38).

Before Jesus ascended to heaven, He gave His disciples some clear instructions: "And being assembled together with them, He commanded them not to depart from Jerusalem, but to wait for the Promise of the Father, 'which,' He said, 'you have heard from Me; for John truly baptized with water, but you shall be baptized with the Holy Spirit not many days from now'" (Acts 1:4-5).

Jesus had been preparing them for His departure for some time now, all the while pointing to "another Helper" who would come to take His place. The disciples still were not sure what He was talking about so they asked a political question about restoring the kingdom to Israel. That's when Jesus said, "But you shall receive *power* when the Holy Spirit has come upon you; and you shall be witnesses to Me in Jerusalem, and in all Judea and Samaria, and to the end of the earth" (Acts 1:8, emphasis added).

The disciples were to receive the same power that had flowed through Jesus, and they were not to begin their ministry without it. They had been a witness to the teachings, life, miracles, death, and resurrection of Jesus. They had even been sent out to do some preaching and healing of their own. They now understood that the Christ had to suffer and die for the sins of the world, and they had received the commission to make disciples of all nations. But there was still something missing.

The Bible says that the church waited and prayed for ten days for this promised Holy Spirit baptism. And then came Pentecost.

When the Day of Pentecost had fully come, they were all with one accord in one place. And suddenly there came a sound from heaven, as of a rushing mighty wind, and it filled the whole house where they were sitting. Then there appeared to them divided tongues, as of fire, and one sat upon each of them. And they were all filled with the Holy Spirit and began to speak with other tongues, as the Spirit gave them utterance. (Acts 2:1-4)

This event was an invasion of heaven to earth, and after this explosive experience with the power of God, the church began to advance in dramatic ways. That very day three thousand people came to the Lord. Miracles became commonplace. Boldness filled the apostles in the face of great persecution. The presence and power of God was so strong that outsiders were actually afraid to join the believers, and yet God added to the church daily (see Acts 5:12-16).

The Purpose of Pentecost

At this point a very clear distinction needs to be made. Although a valid argument can be made for speaking in tongues as the initial evidence of the baptism of the Holy Spirit, tongues is not the only purpose of the baptism. The purpose of Pentecost is power. Power to set captives free. Power to heal the sick. Power to be a witness. Power to minister as Jesus did. The word that Jesus used for power is the Greek word *dunamis.* "You will receive *dunamis* when the Holy Spirit comes upon you." This word refers to supernatural miraculous power and is even often translated as the word "miracles" in the New Testament.

Jesus made it very clear. He did not say, "You will receive tongues when the Holy Spirit comes upon you," He said, "You will receive power." I have a high value for speaking in tongues. It is a very valuable gift from the Lord and in no way should be discredited or diminished. But if we reduce the baptism of the Holy Spirit to speaking in tongues only, we will be satisfied with having a prayer language even if we are not operating in spiritual power. This confusion between the evidence and the purpose of the baptism of the Spirit has caused many who speak in tongues to stop pursuing ongoing impartations of power from on high.

It is very common to have churches where many people in the congregation speak in tongues, and still the overall atmosphere of the church is void of the power of God. There is little or no manifestation of the gifts of the Spirit and not much in the way of healing and deliverance. My experiences with some charismatic/Pentecostal churches have been disheartening in that besides their doctrinal statements, there has really not been much difference between them and churches that don't believe in the gifts and power of God for today. Correct belief about the gifts is not enough. Speaking in tongues is not enough. We need to be clothed with power!

I cannot be satisfied with believing in the gifts of the Spirit but not experiencing them. I cannot be satisfied with knowing that healing is for today but not see miracles happening through me or around me. Therefore, I am constantly pressing into God for a fresh impartation of His power. This in fact is the pattern of the book of Acts. They had ongoing encounters with the Holy Spirit beyond their experience on the day of Pentecost. Peter for example, was filled with the Holy Spirit three separate times in the first four chapters of Acts (see Acts 2:4, Acts 4:8, and Acts 4:31).

In my own journey I have seen definite measures of increase in the anointing and power of the Holy Spirit upon my life and ministry. I am also well aware that I have much more to receive, and I think we should always have a healthy hunger for more. When I first got married, I was a teacher at a Christian school. During this time the Lord led me to set aside extra prayer time each day for ten days for the specific purpose of waiting on Him for the power of the Spirit. During those times I would do nothing but meditate on passages concerning the power of the Spirit and wait in God's presence asking and believing for an increase in power.

After the tenth day, I prayed for a student whose one leg was shorter than the other by about an inch and a half. The short leg grew out before our eyes as I commanded it to grow in the name of Jesus. Soon after this miracle there was an outbreak of other miracles including the healing of a rotator cuff, a broken wrist, a sprained knee, and an injured neck. Along with these healings there were several instances of students being delivered from evil spirits. During this time there was such expectancy that each day I would wonder what God was going to do next!

Impartation

Impartation is an interesting and somewhat controversial subject in the body of Christ today. I define impartation as a reception of supernatural power from God that brings a definite positive difference in a person's life and/or ministry. Oftentimes impartation refers to receiving a spiritual gift or a specific anointing. An example would be having someone lay hands on you in prayer and then subsequently having a prophetic anointing in dreams and visions that previously was not there. Another example would be having a healing evangelist lay hands on you and noticing a definite increase in the healing anointing following this prayer.

Some would question whether this practice has any scriptural foundation, but there is a clear biblical precedent in both the Old and New Testament. In the Old Testament Joshua received an impartation from Moses: "Now Joshua the son of Nun was full of the spirit of wisdom, *for Moses had laid his hands on him*" (Deuteronomy 34:9, emphasis added). In the New Testament Paul told Timothy to "stir up the gift of God which is in you *through the laying on of my hands*" (2 Timothy 1:6, emphasis added). There are other examples in the Bible that affirm the reality that the power of the Holy Spirit can be imparted through the laying on of hands (Acts 8:14-20 and Acts 19:6 are good examples).

We must actively and relentlessly pursue being continually filled with the power of God's Spirit. There seems to be two primary ways of receiving a fresh baptism of power, or impartation; the laying on of hands, as seen above, and waiting on the Lord in prayer. As I have studied about the lives of men and women who have been used mightily by God, I have noticed something: the main common denominator in all of their lives was an emphasis on prayer. They could have different denominational backgrounds and different beliefs about certain doctrines, but they were all people of much prayer. I further noticed that many of them practiced something they called *waiting on God* which refers to being still before God in prayer. I believe that this is a significant spiritual discipline and one of the keys to maintaining a lifestyle of intimacy and power in the Holy Spirit.

If you desire to operate in the supernatural ministry of Jesus, find a trustworthy person who is already doing it, and spend as much time with them as you can. Have them lay hands on you and ask God to impart a fresh anointing upon your life. Then, spend time waiting in God's presence, asking for the power of the Spirit to become a greater reality in your life. Whatever you do, do not settle for less than being clothed with the Spirit's power!

Obstacles to the Pursuit of Power

Christianity without power does not exist in the New Testament. Unfortunately, for the most part we have so accepted it as the norm today that anyone operating in the power of God is seen as extreme. There are several obstacles that can hinder a person or church from pursuing a ministry of power.

Fear of Being Unbalanced

Some are afraid that if they begin to pursue miraculous ministry, they or their church will take it too far and become unbalanced.

The truth is, those who subscribe to this type of thinking are already unbalanced, extremely unbalanced. Jesus spent at least as much time and energy healing the sick and casting out demons as He did teaching and preaching. If we are to be truly biblically balanced in our churches, we will do the same.

You would be hard pressed to find a church today that is exclusively given to healing and deliverance ministry without making any room for teaching or preaching. I highly doubt that such a church exists. On the other hand, there are multitudes of churches that have an abundance of teaching without any time given at all to healing or freeing captives. If balance is what we are looking for (and true, biblical balance is a good thing), then let's be honest with ourselves and realize that much of what we call balanced is terribly lopsided according to the example of Jesus.

Fear of Deception

As I have discussed the topic of healing and deliverance with others, I have been amazed that many people ignore the example and commands of Jesus to heal the sick and cast out demons based on the passage where Jesus warns about deception and false prophets in Matthew 7:15-23. Using this logic, Moses would have refused to perform the signs that God commanded him, because the Egyptian sorcerers were doing the same things (see Exodus 7:8-12). As ridiculous as that may sound, that is exactly what many are doing today.

It is no secret that counterfeits exist, and this fact should not alarm us. The devil will always imitate and pervert the power of God. Sadly, many people who are involved in the occult and Satanism are operating in more spiritual power than many Christians. Not only that, but countless churches would not have the capability to help such people out of their bondage should they desire freedom. A problem occurs when we react in fear instead of responding to truth. It is amazing how the devil can use our fear of a bad thing to keep us from pursuing a good thing.

Discernment is extremely important, and we must certainly take the commands of Scripture that warn us to be aware of deception seriously. But we cannot afford to build a theology that opposes the work of the Spirit, because we are afraid of being deceived. True discernment is not based on a fear of deception but on a love of the truth. And according to Jesus, true discernment requires us to not only know the Scriptures but to also know the power of God (see Matthew 22:29).

The Either/or Fallacy

Another objection to the power of God is the false idea that we are somehow forced to choose between character or power; fruit of the Spirit or gifts of the Spirit. Some say, "Well, love is the most important thing, so I am going to just love people." Or "Paul said that without love the gifts of the Spirit are meaningless" (see 1 Corinthians 13). Or "Who cares about having power if we are not living in holiness." While I understand the sentiment behind these statements, nowhere in the Bible does it say that we must choose between fruit and gifts or between love and power. What it does say however is "Pursue love, *and* desire spiritual gifts" (1 Corinthians 14:1, emphasis added). We do not have the right to put an *or* where God has put an *and*. Both character and power are essential to the ministry of Jesus. They are not in opposition to each other and nor do we have to choose between the two.

One possible reason for this misunderstanding is the difference between how fruit and gifts function. Fruit must be cultivated over time while gifts can be received in an instant. This makes it possible to walk in great power and gifting without exhibiting mature character. We have seen examples of this in our times and there are also biblical examples. While some will stumble over this seeming dissonance, we must simply accept it as reality and learn to walk in gifting while continuing to grow in love and character.

God wants to express Himself to the world, and that's why He has given us the fruit and gifts of the Spirit. The fruit express His nature and the gifts His power. Don't choose between the two— God never said you had to.

Wrong Theology

The church I grew up in held to what is called *cessationist* theology. This type of theology states that the sign gifts of the Holy Spirit such as tongues, healings, miracles, and prophecy have ceased and are no longer to be a part of the Christian experience or church life. As the story goes, now that we have the completed Bible, we no longer need such demonstrations of power. If your only Christian experience was in such a church setting, you might come to the conclusion that cessationist theology is correct, because typically the Holy Spirit does not manifest Himself and move in power where He is not welcomed.

As I began my pursuit of God at age 19, I began to wonder about these things called the gifts of the Spirit. I immediately came to the conclusion that if they were for today, we were missing something very important in our church. And based on the Scriptures, I had to conclude that they were for today, and I began to "eagerly desire spiritual gifts" (1 Corinthians 14:1). It would have been more comfortable for me to just sweep the gifts under the proverbial rug and carry on with life as before. Then I wouldn't have to wonder why I hadn't experienced such manifestations of power or why my church had failed to inform me about them. It would have been an easy answer to my questions about why things seemed so different compared to the Bible.

If you ever have to choose between comfort and truth, choose truth every time. The truth is, there is not a single shred of biblical evidence to back up a Christianity without supernatural power, however uncomfortable that may make us. There is no true biblical basis for cessationist doctrine.

A Naturalistic Mindset

A naturalistic mindset, or world-view, is one that explains everything in natural terms and is extremely skeptical of anything supernatural. This is the pervasive mindset of the Western culture and it has no doubt influenced the church greatly. As a result, the supernatural elements of Christianity are largely considered to be irrelevant for us today. While those of a liberal theology would deny both the miracles of the Bible and miracles for today, most evangelicals will affirm strongly the miracles of the Bible. But they tend to spiritualize them so that their application for us today doesn't encourage us to expect such things to happen here and now.

Because of this naturalistic mindset, secular techniques are often employed for ministry. A clear example is in the area of counseling those with mental or emotional problems. If we only view these issues from a natural perspective, we will end up using psychological tactics to deal with problems that have spiritual roots. While not every problem is caused by demons, if a demon is the problem, deliverance is the answer. You can't counsel away a demon!

The Problem of Unbelief

All of the above oppositions have a common root of unbelief, and unbelief has a quick way of extinguishing the work of the Holy Spirit. Look at what happened when Jesus ran into unbelief in His hometown of Nazareth. "Now He could do no mighty work there, except that He laid His hands on a few sick people and healed them. And He marveled because of their unbelief" (Mark 6:5-6). The environment of unbelief severely hindered Christ to the point that He could not do many miracles. The passage makes it clear that it was not because of the will of God, but because of the lack of faith and the lack of honor given to Jesus that more miracles did not happen.

I believe that much of the Western church is similar to Nazareth. We see much less of the supernatural power of God than other parts of the world, because we are shrouded in an atmosphere of skepticism and unbelief. Thankfully, God is breaking through, and we are beginning to see more and more of the miraculous works of Jesus take place. There are some churches where it is now common for miracles to take place on a weekly basis, and the miracles are not only increasing in number but also in notability. Healing of cancer, multiple sclerosis, deafness, and other serious illnesses are becoming increasingly common, although there is still much territory to be contended for.

We must seriously confront our unbelief and admit how far off we truly are from walking in Christ's ministry. Then, we must contend for our promised land. It is okay to be far away from walking in the fullness of God's promises as long as you are aggressively moving in their direction. What is not okay is being satisfied with the status quo and remaining where you are. God is raising up a generation of believers who walk in His authority and are clothed with His power. Will you be a part of this generation?

8

Intimacy with the Father

In the previous chapter we saw that the ministry of Jesus was empowered by the Holy Spirit. Now we will turn our attention to the fact that this power for ministry flowed out of an intimate relationship with the Father.

Before launching into His ministry, Jesus was baptized by John the Baptist. The heavens were opened to Him, the Holy Spirit came upon Him, and the voice of the Father spoke over Him: "This is My beloved Son, in whom I am well pleased" (see Matthew 3:16-17). What is important to note is that God the Father declared His love and approval for His Son *before* He started His ministry. Before one sermon was preached, one sick person was healed, or one demon was cast out, Jesus received the Father's blessing.

Jesus was not working *for* the Father's love but *from* the Father's love. There is a huge difference between the two. His ministry was not an effort to gain approval but an outflow of His intimate relationship with the Father. He did not need to perform in order to be loved; He was perfectly loved already. Love was the foundation for what He did, not the thing He strived to gain.

Jesus' whole life and ministry flowed from the place of intimacy with God. This was the root system beneath the surface that gave life to the tree above. Consider the following verses:

> Then Jesus answered and said to them, "Most assuredly, I say to you, the Son can do nothing of Himself, but what He sees the Father do; for whatever He does, the Son also does in like manner. For the Father loves the Son, and shows Him all things that He Himself does; and He will show Him greater works than these, that you may marvel." (John 5:19-20)

> I can of Myself do nothing. As I hear, I judge; and My judgment is righteous, because I do not seek My own will but the will of the Father who sent Me. (John 5:30)

In these passages Jesus speaks of both seeing and hearing what the Father is doing. The picture is of an intimate relationship where the Father is leading Jesus every step of the way. It is also significant that Jesus tied this intimacy with the miracles He was doing by saying "and He will show Him greater works than these, that you may marvel." This relationship between intimacy and power is also seen in a statement made in Daniel 11:32: "the people who know their God shall be strong, and carry out great exploits." While it is surprisingly possible for false prophets to carry out great exploits without knowing God (see Matthew 7:21-23), it is also clear that those who do know God should be doing great exploits.

All true ministry flows out of intimacy with God. The cross reconciles us to God, restoring us to a right relationship with Him. We're saved *from* hell and sin but also saved *into* fellowship with

God. It would change our perspective to understand that eternal life does not only refer to going to heaven when we die but also to intimately knowing God here and now (see John 17:3).

The foundation of our intimacy with God is His love. I believe that we can only grow as close to God as our present revelation of His love for us. God's love is declared to us in His Word and demonstrated to us by the cross, but we often have trouble receiving this love until we truly encounter it in a personal way. Jesus came to reveal who the Father is to the world. When He healed somebody, it was not just a demonstration of power; it was also a demonstration of the Father's love. Every time we experience the love of the Father in a personal way, it is an invitation to draw into a deeper relationship with Him.

As we discuss different elements of growing in intimacy with God, it is important that we remember this foundation of His love for us. Remember, "We love Him because He first loved us" (1 John 4:19). Our love for God is a response to His love for us.

The Place of Prayer

Not only can Christ's closeness to the Father be seen in His being led moment by moment, it can also be seen in His prayer life. A survey of the gospels will show the prominent place that Jesus gave to prayer.

One example is Mark 1:35 which reads, "Now in the morning, having risen a long while before daylight, He went out and departed to a solitary place; and there He prayed." What makes this verse so amazing is the context in which it is stated. In the preceding verses (21-34) we read of an intense day of ministry including teaching and casting out a demon in a synagogue, healing Peter's mother-in-law, and ministering healing and deliverance to crowds of people who came to Him in the evening. Before having children, my wife and I had the tradition of taking a Sunday nap each week after church. But I don't think that Jesus had time for a "Sabbath nap" that day—He was up well into the night in exhausting ministry. But "in the morning...a long while before daylight...He prayed."

While many people view prayer as a last resort, this passage shows that Jesus saw it as a top priority. He needed to be in prayer; interceding, receiving direction, and just being in the presence of His Father. Luke 5:16 sums it up well: "So He Himself often withdrew into the wilderness and prayed." This was not a once-in-a while event but a regular practice. In the midst of the demands of a busy traveling ministry, Jesus could often be found alone with God. This is a great example for all of us. The secret to a life of intimacy with God is spending much time in the secret place of His presence. This is one element that cannot be ignored, and the fuller our schedule gets, the more intentional we must be. An expanding public influence with a shrinking secret place is a recipe for disaster.

The disciples were also called to a place of intimacy. Take a close look at the calling of the twelve apostles: "Then He appointed twelve, *that they might be with Him* and that He might send them out to preach, and to have power to heal sicknesses and to cast out demons" (Mark 3:14-15, emphasis added). Their first assignment was to be with Jesus. Their training for ministry was not Bible school or seminary; it was the presence of Jesus. All other ministry was to flow out of that relationship. We too must learn to constantly spend time in the presence of God.

While it takes discipline to have a consistent prayer life, discipline is not the goal. Instead, discipline becomes the gateway to an intimate relationship with God. Intimacy is the goal and the highest purpose of prayer. This principle of discipline applies to human relationships as well. My wife and I have certain things, such as regular date nights and times of praying together, which we do on a consistent basis to help maintain and grow in intimacy with each other. We have learned that as our lives get busier, we have to become intentional and disciplined in order to continue these practices. Again, discipline is not the goal but a means to deeper relationship.

Prayer is spending time with God, and you cannot get to know someone with whom you do not spend time. I encourage you to spend quality time with God every day in prayer and reading His Word, not out of a legalistic performance but out of a desire for God Himself. We should come to God in prayer not to become accepted by Him but because we have already been accepted by Him. These two practices of prayer and Bible study are the foundation for all other spiritual growth and lead to increasing intimacy with the Father.

Along with focused time with God, learning to converse with Him throughout the day will also increase intimacy with Him and will heighten our awareness of His presence. Quality time with God can be compared to having dinner with your spouse. Communing throughout the day with Him is like having short phone calls or sending text messages to your spouse. Both quality time and constant communion help cultivate intimacy.

The Manifest Presence

A key for growing in intimacy with the Father is having a sincere hunger for His presence. The Bible teaches us that God is omnipresent which means that His presence is everywhere. But we must also understand that there is a difference between the *omnipresence* of God and the *manifest presence* of God. God's manifest presence is His presence revealed to us in a tangible way; it is His experiential presence. His omnipresence means He is everywhere; His manifest presence means He is *here*. When I speak of experiencing the manifest presence of God, I am not referring to an emotional feeling, though sometimes emotions are involved. It is something tangible and is totally apart from ourselves, though we get to enter into it.

I have heard it said that since God is everywhere we should not speak in terms such as God showing up in a meeting, church service, or prayer time. But this type of thinking fails to distinguish between these two types of God's presence. For example, while everyone in Jerusalem was in the omnipresence of God on the day of Pentecost, only those in the upper room came into contact with His manifest presence. His presence came as a rushing wind, tongues of fire, and the supernatural experience of speaking in tongues. Certainly, God showed up! We should have a continual hunger and thirst for the manifest presence of God.

Moses was a man who was familiar with the manifest presence of God. While talking with the Lord about entering the Promised Land he said, "If Your Presence does not go with us, do not bring us up from here" (Exodus 33:15). That is the kind of hunger that God is looking for today. Moses preferred to be in the wilderness with God rather than to be in the Promised Land without Him. Let's remember this important principle as we contend for our own spiritual promised land. It is so easy to get caught up in the promises and blessings of God and lose sight of the purpose of it all: *to know Him.*

I remember when I first began to experience the tangible presence of God. I was a junior in college and had been crying out to God for more of His presence and power. I had read the accounts of past revivalists such as Charles Finney and was hungry to experience more of God. One particular night I was crying out to God for more of Him and mediating on Ezekiel 47:1-12 where Ezekiel had a prophetic encounter in which he was led into a river. At first the water was up to his ankles, then to his knees, then to his waist, and finally it was so deep that he could not stand up in it any longer. So, I was specifically praying for God to take me deeper into His river based on that passage.

The next morning, I woke up and began to spend time with the Lord. But as soon as I started praying, I felt a tangible presence come over my feet. I paused to ask the Lord what this was and was immediately reminded of Ezekiel 47. I was up to the ankle. Later that day I spent time in prayer and the same sensation came upon my feet, but this time it began to travel up my legs to my knees. God had answered my prayers for more of His presence in a specific and personal way, and I have been experiencing the manifest presence of God in various ways ever since that encounter.

The Veil is Torn

One of my favorite Bible passages is Mark 15:37-38 which reads, "And Jesus cried out with a loud voice, and breathed His last. Then the veil of the temple was torn in two from top to bottom." I love this passage because it clearly illustrates the unlimited access that we now have to the manifest presence of God.

The veil that was torn in the temple was a thick curtain that separated the Holy Place from the Most Holy Place (also called the Holy of Holies). The Holy of Holies was the place where God's actual tangible presence dwelt in the temple. Only the high priest was permitted to enter into this place and only one time per year. As soon as Jesus died on the cross, this veil was torn from top to bottom giving us entrance into God's immediate presence. Hebrews 10:19-22 reads:

> Therefore, brothers, since we have confidence to enter the Most Holy Place by the blood of Jesus, by a new and living way opened for us through the curtain, that is, his body, and since we have a great priest over the house of God, let us draw near to God with a sincere heart in full assurance of faith, having our hearts sprinkled to cleanse us from a

guilty conscience and having our bodies washed with pure water.

Because of the cross, every one of us can enter into the Most Holy Place of His presence at any time. Consider what a profound thought that is in light of how limited the access was under the Old Covenant. We are exhorted to draw near to God with the promise that He will then draw near to us (see James 4:8). Every Christian can and should experience the manifest presence of God. Each person's experience with God's presence will be different, but we can all experience it. Like David, begin to seek the face of God and thirst for His presence, and you will find that He truly rewards those who diligently seek Him.

God's Voice

Another aspect of growing in intimacy with God is learning to recognize His voice. Jesus was constantly guided by the voice of His Father and said that we would have the same privilege: "My sheep hear My voice, and I know them, and they follow Me" (John 10:27). Christianity is a relationship and that means there should be two-way communication. Not only does God want us to speak to Him, He wants to return the favor. Throughout the Bible we see that God was always speaking to people in various ways. Below are some of the ways that God may speak to *you*.

The Bible

The primary way that God speaks to us is through the Bible. This may be through reading passages on your own, Bible study with others, or hearing preaching or teaching from the Word. The Bible provides the foundation for our walk with God but is not the only way that He communicates with us. Some think that since we have the Bible, we do not need other ways to hear from God, but the Bible itself teaches that we are to be led by the Holy Spirit (see

Romans 8:14). While the Bible gives us general promises, commands, and teachings that apply to all believers, the Spirit can give us specific guidance that relates to our personal lives. For example, God's Word teaches us general principles about marriage, but the Holy Spirit can lead us to who we should marry. The Bible does not tell you who to marry, what job to take, where to live, what your individual calling is, and so on. We need to become familiar with the voice of God.

In Acts 16 the apostle Paul was obeying the general command to preach the gospel when he was "forbidden by the Holy Spirit to preach the word in Asia" (Acts 16:6). He then tried to go to Mysia and was also denied by the Spirit. Eventually God spoke to Paul in a vision and led him to preach in Macedonia (see Acts 16:6-10). Like Paul, we need to obey the clear commands of Scripture and seek to follow God's ways while also being in tune with His Spirit and the other ways in which He speaks.

As we look at some of these other ways, keep in mind that anything that God says to you will be in line with the overall counsel of His Word and will never contradict it.

The Still, Small Voice

This may come in the form of an impression, gentle whisper, or a quiet nudge of the Holy Spirit. I was in prayer one morning when I felt like the Spirit was prompting me to write my wife a note before I left for work. After my prayer time I wrote her a brief note and put it on the countertop for her to see when she woke up. Later she called me, thanked me for the note, and said that the first thought in her mind that morning was, *It would be nice if Jake wrote me a note today.* God is so personal! Pay attention to the subtle ways His still, small voice will come to you.

The Audible Voice

There are times in the Bible when God spoke with an audible voice for all to hear. One example is when Jesus was praying at a time shortly before going to the cross: "Then a voice came from heaven, saying, 'I have both glorified it and will glorify it again'" (John 12:28). Although God's audible voice seems to be a rarer experience, I personally know a few people who have heard the audible voice of God and have heard the testimony of many others who have as well.

Dreams and Visions

While not every dream we have is from God, it is clear from the Bible that God uses dreams to speak to us. In the Old Testament Joseph had dreams that forecasted his destiny of being a ruler one day. Jacob had a powerful encounter with God in a dream where he saw an open heaven and a ladder with angels ascending and descending. There are plenty of other examples in both the Old and New Testament. I have had certain dreams that I knew were from God like the one I shared in Chapter Six that called me into the ministry of deliverance.

A vision is seeing something with our spiritual eyes. It can range from a mental picture to an open-eyed vision to a trancelike state where we are basically dreaming while awake (see Acts 10:9-11). According to the prophet Joel, dreams and visions are to increase in the last days (see Joel 2:28-32).

Angels

Hebrews 1:14 says that angels are "ministering spirits sent forth to minister for those who will inherit salvation." One of the ways that angels minister is to bring messages from God to His people. It was the angel Gabriel who visited Mary and told her of the coming Messiah that she was to bring forth into the world. An angel spoke to Phillip in Acts 8:26 and told him of a specific street he was to go to where he would lead someone to the Lord. Angels can appear in human form or in a glorious form. Either way, let's be aware of these messengers of God and ask God to send His angels on our behalf.

Other People

God will often use other people to speak to us. This can come through preaching, the gifts of the Spirit (such as prophecy), regular conversation, or many other ways. A person may not even realize that what they are saying is actually the voice of God to us for that moment. We should be open to how God may speak to us through others.

I'll never forget the time God used my sister to speak to me while I was in an intense season of spiritual attack. I was praying one night and asking God to speak to me and give me a word concerning the situation. As soon as I said "Amen," my phone beeped with a text message from my sister that simply said, "2 Thessalonians 3:3." I looked up the verse and found these words: "But the Lord is faithful, who will establish you and guard you from the evil one." This was a tremendous encouragement to me and a sure weapon against the enemy's assaults. The next day I asked my sister, who knew nothing of the spiritual battle I was in, why she had texted me that verse. She said that the Holy Spirit had come upon her and she began to intercede in tongues, knowing that she was praying for me. As she continued to pray, God spoke that Scripture reference to her and she sent it to me. He is faithful!

Any Other Way He Wants

There is no exhaustive list of how God may speak to us. The above list is a good start and some of the ways that seem to be most common, but God is God and can speak to us in any way that He chooses. He once spoke to a man through the lips of a donkey (see

RESTORING THE MINISTRY OF JESUS

Numbers 22:28). He can speak to us through our circumstances and trials, through nature and creation, and countless other ways. Just when we think we have God figured out He will speak to us in a completely new way. I once heard the voice of God through a T-shirt that a random person was wearing at a coffee shop. At other times He has used a pattern of seeing the same numbers over and over again to speak and confirm His voice and direction.

The key to all of this is growing in intimacy with the Father. If we are going to do what Jesus did and walk like Jesus walked, we will need to become more and more acquainted with the voice of God. I certainly do not speak about the voice of God flippantly or claim to have a constant flow of words from God, but I want to increase in my sensitivity to His voice so that I can be in tune with heaven and release God's kingdom into the world around me. I want to know His voice, because I want to know Him.

Mary's Example

The Christian walk is a relationship with God above all else. The religious spirit turns the Christian walk into a list of rules or a set of beliefs. Don't get me wrong; we need correct beliefs and proper guidelines. But that is not the point of it all. The gospel of Luke tells of a woman named Mary who understood the priority of intimacy with Jesus. She serves as a great example of one who longed for the presence and voice of God. Look at Luke 10:38-42:

> Now it happened as they went that He entered a certain village; and a certain woman named Martha welcomed Him into her house. And she had a sister called Mary, who also sat at Jesus' feet and heard His word. But Martha was distracted with much serving, and she approached Him and said, "Lord, do You not care that my sister has left me to serve alone? Therefore tell her to help me." And Jesus answered and said to her, "Martha, Martha, you are

worried and troubled about many things. But one thing is needed, and Mary has chosen that good part, which will not be taken away from her."

Martha invited Jesus into her home, but Mary made Him the center of attention. Martha was busy serving. Serving is great but not when it is time to be in the presence of God, focused on Him. Notice that the text calls her serving a *distraction*. I have found that if the devil can't get you distracted with sinning, he will try to get you distracted with serving. This takes on an even deeper meaning when we realize that the same word for serving in the original Greek language can also be translated as *ministering*. If we become preoccupied with the demands of life, serving, or ministry, to the exclusion of our time in the secret place, we are cutting ourselves off from the very source of life and fruitfulness. This is a dangerous place to be.

Mary on the other hand was captivated by the Lord's presence and by His voice. She sat at His feet and listened to His every word. When Martha complained to Jesus, He responded by telling her that only one thing is needed and that Mary had chosen that one thing. The one thing that is needed is to intimately know God, because everything else will flow out of that.

It is time to become a people of His presence, a people who seek His face above all else. The top priority of a Christian is to be with Jesus and to truly know Him. Are you content with your present level of intimacy with God, or do you hunger to know Him more? Are you satisfied with how you hear His voice and experience His presence? Are you content to live in the outer courts, or do you long for the Holy of Holies? Are you interested simply in what God has, or do you desire to know Him for who He is?

God is looking for more than servants, He is looking for friends. He desires relationship, not just people to do things for Him. This does not mean that we are not to serve God but that there is something more than serving, which is to know Him and walk with Him. Restoring the ministry of Jesus means more than preaching, seeing miracles, and casting out demons. We can only make God known to others to the level that we truly know Him. As we become more intimate with Him, His love and goodness will flow out of our lives as a byproduct. As we seek to restore the ministry of Jesus, let's remember that the first call of the disciples was to be with Him. If we miss this then we miss everything!

9

Broken Vessels

If we are going to walk like Jesus walked and do what Jesus did, we must establish the value of seeking His face and growing in intimacy with Him. Jesus said that unless we abide in Him, we will not produce any lasting fruit for the kingdom. Like a branch is dependent upon its connection to the vine, so are we dependent on our connection to Christ (see John 15:4-5). Along with intimacy, there is another quality that will help us to truly walk in the ministry of Jesus and that is *brokenness.*

Being a Broken Vessel

And being in Bethany at the house of Simon the leper, as He sat at the table, a woman came having an alabaster

flask of very costly oil of spikenard. Then she broke the
flask and poured it on His head. (Mark 14:3)

Based on John's version of this story found in John 12:1-8, the
woman who poured this costly oil onto Jesus was Mary, the sister
of Lazarus whom Jesus raised from the dead. This is the same Mary
that we saw in the previous chapter who sat at the Lord's feet while
her sister Martha was distracted with serving. Though the others
criticized her for her lavish display of affection towards Jesus, Mary
was keenly aware of something that the others were missing: *the
worth of Jesus*. She knew that He was worth it. It was worth it for her
to "waste" a year's wages in pouring this costly oil onto Jesus. It
was worth it for her to sit at the Lord's feet, giving Him her undivided time and attention. It was worth it, because He is worthy.

There was nothing too special about the flask itself except that
it carried such expensive and precious oil inside of it. Before the oil
could be poured upon Jesus and the sweet fragrance fill the room,
the flask had to be broken. Christians are much the same way. We
"have this treasure in earthen vessels" (2 Corinthians 4:7). In and of
ourselves we are weak and fragile, but we carry in us the treasure
of heaven. Christ lives in us. We are the temple of the Holy Spirit.
But just like Mary's flask, until *we are broken* the treasure remains
inside of us and the fragrance of Christ does not fill the world
around us.

Christ desires to live through us by the power of the Holy Spirit.
I think we take statements like this too lightly. Consider these
verses of Scripture: "To them God willed to make known what are
the riches of the glory of this mystery among the Gentiles: *which is
Christ in you, the hope of glory*" (Colossians 1:27, Emphasis added).
"Do you not know that *your body is a temple of the Holy Spirit*, who is
in you, whom you have received from God?" (1 Corinthians 6:19,
emphasis added). It is an incredibly profound concept that God

would live inside of imperfect people, and I think that we have heard these things so often that it has lost its wonder.

If God lives in me and in every other Christian, then shouldn't things look a little different in our lives and in the life of the church? Shouldn't there be more love? Shouldn't there be more holiness? Shouldn't there be more power? Think about it; *God Himself* lives inside of us! The answer to these questions is yes. I believe that we have only scratched the surface to the potential of the Christian life modeled to us by Jesus.

One reason that there is not more of Christ's love and power flowing through our lives is that we often remain unbroken vessels. The fragrant oil is in the jar, but the jar is unbroken.

You Give them Something to Eat!

In the story of Jesus feeding the five thousand, there are some keys to walking in the ministry of Jesus, including the role that brokenness plays.

When the day was now far spent, His disciples came to Him and said, "This is a deserted place, and already the hour is late. Send them away, that they may go into the surrounding country and villages and buy themselves bread; for they have nothing to eat." But He answered and said to them, "You give them something to eat." And they said to Him, "Shall we go and buy two hundred denarii worth of bread and give them something to eat?" But He said to them, "How many loaves do you have? Go and see." And when they found out they said, "Five, and two fish." Then He commanded them to make them all sit down in groups on the green grass. So they sat down in ranks, in hundreds and in fifties. And when He had taken the five loaves and the two fish, He looked up to heaven, blessed and broke the loaves, and gave them to His disciples to set before them; and the two fish He divided among them all. So they all ate and were filled. And they took up twelve baskets full of fragments and of the fish. Now those who had eaten the loaves were about five thousand men. (Mark 6:35-44)

Coupled with Matthew's version of this same incident in Matthew 14:13-21, I believe that this passage gives us an awesome picture of how God wants to use us to minister to and bless multitudes of people. I do not necessarily mean ministering to thousands of people at one time but rather over the course of our lives. I like to break this story down into six progressive steps to illustrate this process of being used by God in the ministry of Jesus.

1. See That There Is a Problem

The disciples came to Jesus with a problem: it was getting late and the multitudes of people had nothing to eat. The people were hungry for the Word of God, apparently so hungry that they neglected to bring food with them into this deserted region. Whether or not the disciples were genuinely concerned for the wellbeing of the people we do not know; in fact, their motives may have been questionable. The twelve had just returned from a "mission trip" that consisted of preaching the kingdom, healing the sick, and driving demons out of people, and had actually gone into this deserted place to get some much-needed rest. However, thousands of needy people followed them and Jesus began to minister to them. Dismissing the people to get food could very well have been a convenient way of getting rid of the crowd that was hindering their desire for relaxation.

Whether or not their motives were 100% pure (and I suspect they were not), the disciples recognized a genuine problem and brought it to Jesus. This is the first step in being used by God: recognizing a problem or need; and we won't have to look very far to find one. This world is not the way that God originally created it to be. Everywhere you look there are lost souls, sicknesses, people in torment, trauma and abuse, widows and orphans, and those with no food. There is occult darkness and sexual immorality, murder, theft, and other crimes. But we must *see* the need. We can be so pre-occupied with our own little world that we neglect the needs around us. In John 4:35 Jesus said to His disciples, "lift up your eyes and look at the fields, for they are already white for harvest!" We need to see the harvest!

2. Recognize our Responsibility in Being Part of the Solution

Once we see a problem, our initial response is often to run to God and ask Him to fix it. But notice the response of Jesus: "You give them something to eat" (vs. 37). *You* fix it. *You* take care of this problem. *You* give them something to eat. The disciples must have been dumbfounded. Not only was this not getting rid of the crowd, it was increasing their workload and giving them an assignment that was absolutely impossible to fulfill!

This is a great example of how we frequently treat the needs of our day; we just want God to fix everything with little or no cost to ourselves. We want God to save the lost, but we don't preach the gospel, travail in intercession, or reach out with compassion. We would love for God to alleviate poverty, but we live and spend self-ishly. We hope for God to set people free instead of using our God-given authority to deliver the captives. We complain about the darkness, failing to realize that *we* are supposed to be the light of the world (see Matthew 5:14-16). God is saying, "*You* give them something to eat."

The fact of the matter is, God works on this planet through hu-man beings. In His sovereignty He has made it to be that way. He has given us the privilege and responsibility to partner with Him through our prayers and obedience to see His will accomplished on earth. Did you ever realize that your steps of obedience will be the answer to someone's prayers? Yes, there are people waiting on the other side of your obedience. We need to see our responsibility and step into the areas that God calls us. The needs of earth are great, and the supply of heaven is more than enough. The link that brings heaven to earth is you and me. *You* give them something to eat.

3. Acknowledge our own Lack

Once we see the problem and accept responsibility for being a part of the solution, we have two options: we can either acknowledge our absolute inability to solve the problem or we can forge ahead in our own strength. How did the disciples respond? "We have here only five loaves and two fish" (Matthew 14:17). In other words, they acknowledged their lack. You can try to feed five thousand men (plus women and children) with five loaves and two fish, but you won't get very far. In fact, you will hardly begin to make a dent in fixing the problem.

This is how it is with us today as well. Many people get through steps one and two and then go out in their own strength to solve a problem. The efforts are noble and some good is done, but in the end only a few are fed. For example, it is clear that there are many people living in our world with various torments. Psychology is man's well-meaning effort to help people who are tormented, but without knowledge of the spiritual realm and the power of the Holy Spirit, not many will receive true healing. This holds true for Christian counseling as well as secular. I am not opposed to counseling as a whole, but how much more could be done if we acknowledged our lack and depended on the power of God?

The task of the church is impossible to complete without His supernatural power and intervention. God is often known to give an impossible assignment with the promise of His presence. While God *won't* do it without us, we *can't* do it without Him. This also goes for individual callings. You can see this theme throughout Scripture; God uses weak and unqualified individuals to do impossible tasks by the power of His Spirit. Jesus said, "Without Me you can do nothing" (John 15:5). The good news is that we are not without Him—we must simply learn to rely on Him in complete dependence rather than operating in our own strength.

4. Give What you Have to Jesus

Acknowledging our lack is important, but focusing on our lack is detrimental. There is a big difference. We shouldn't camp out in step three but instead allow it to drive us to dependence on the One who has no lack. Once the disciples recognized that what they had to offer was completely insufficient for the task, they handed over what they had to Jesus (see Matthew 14:18).

We too need to give what we have to Jesus. Jesus is not just our Savior, He is also our Lord. That means that He has a right to rule every area of our lives and to make use of everything that we own. The Bible says that we have been bought with a price, the precious blood of Jesus. Self can no longer be on the throne of our hearts. God will take us through a process of sanctification where He will put His finger on areas of our lives that need to be brought under the lordship of Christ. He will also ask us to lay some things down that may not be sinful in themselves but are starting to take too much priority in our lives.

We need to learn what it means to present our bodies to God as a living sacrifice, giving ourselves totally to Him (see Romans 12:1). I remember kneeling before God during a worship service many years ago and saying, "God, I give myself completely to you so that the multitudes can be fed. I give myself to you so that the lost will be saved, the sick will be healed, and the tormented will be delivered." It is a prayer that I have continued to pray over the years.

Give yourself totally to Jesus so that His ministry can flow through you.

5. Allow God to Bless and Break You

> And when He had taken the five loaves and the two fish, He looked up to heaven, blessed and broke the loaves, and gave them to His disciples to set before them. (Mark 6:41)

Once we give ourselves to Jesus—our gifts and abilities, our dreams, our possessions, and our entire lives—we must then allow Him to bless and break us. The blessing refers to the anointing of the Spirit. As we have already seen, the power of the Holy Spirit was absolutely essential to the ministry of Jesus and will be equally essential to us as we continue in His ministry today. Going without the anointing is going in your own strength.

But not only must we allow God to bless us with His anointing, we must allow Him to break us so that we will have His compassion. The blessing ensures power to serve, while the brokenness ensures purity of motive. It is possible to get through steps one through four with impure motives, but not step five. The disciples came to Jesus wanting to fix the problem of feeding the people, but their inner motives were probably more selfish than anything else. In the same way, we can be zealous to accomplish great things for God while having motives that are primarily self-oriented.

A great example of this is in the area of healing. Desiring a strong anointing for healing and miracles is great but just as important is the question of why we desire such power. God not only cares *that* we heal the sick; He cares *why* we heal the sick. Have you ever considered that? Although there are several great, Christ-centered reasons to pursue a ministry of healing, there can also be some hidden impure motives lurking in the depths of our heart; a desire for fame or money or wanting to prove yourself to others are but a few possibilities. God doesn't anoint us to make us famous, He anoints us to set captives free. That's why He employs the use of brokenness alongside of blessing. As Jesus was moved with compassion when He ministered, He wants our hearts to be moved as well.

Carrying a powerful gift for healing and miracles can easily turn a person into a celebrity in the body of Christ. When the crowds saw the signs and wonders that Jesus did, they tried to make him an earthly king (see John 6:15). When Paul performed a miracle in the city of Lystra, the people called him and Barnabas gods and tried to worship them (see Acts 14:8-13). Are we prepared to handle such temptations that will inevitably accompany the anointing of God? I have come to realize the importance of regularly asking God to examine my motives and to purify me of any form of selfish ambition. When you pray such prayers, be prepared to confront the ugliness in your own heart that is impossible to detect apart from the illumination of the Holy Spirit.

Pride is the deadliest thing to the Christian, and to protect us from it, God often has to break us. The more broken we become, the more the compassion of God and the fragrance of Christ is able to pour out of our lives into the world around us. Like Mary's perfume, the oil of God will then pour through us and touch the lives of those around us in profound ways.

6. Release the Kingdom Through Your Life

The last step in this process is to release the resources of the kingdom of God through your life. These resources include the power of the Holy Spirit, the compassion of Christ, and much more. "So they all ate and were filled" (Mark 6:42). Not one person left without being satisfied. Problem solved. Not only this, but verse 43 goes on to say that there were twelve baskets of leftover food. This clearly teaches us that there is always enough supply in heaven to meet the needs of earth. Whether the problem is sickness, torment, or lack, the kingdom of God has the answer.

We will look more closely at the concept of releasing the kingdom in the final chapter of this book. For now, let's look at how this whole process might look in the example of healing ministry. The first step is to see that there is a great need for healing as many people are suffering from pain, sickness, and disease. Once you see the need, you begin to realize that you are called to do something about it and start to pray for sick people. Soon you begin to recognize your own lack and your complete inability to heal anybody and so you give what you have to Jesus and seek His face like never before. As you give yourself to Jesus, He begins to pour His power on your life and to break your heart so that you have compassion for the sick. Now the kingdom of God begins to be released through your life, and people are being healed by the supernatural power of God.

The Process of Brokenness

The above steps are not meant to be seen as a formulaic path to effective use in the kingdom. Rather, they are meant to give some understanding into the different seasons and situations that you can expect to encounter on your journey to walking in the ministry of Jesus. The above steps are the crucial common elements that we can all expect to go through; however, each person's walk will be unique to themselves as God sees fit.

In my own life, I can look back and see that I have spent time in these different steps. I can remember coming to the realization of the need for people to be set free and the problem of Christians living in bondage and oppression. I recall specific times of deeper consecration, of saying yes to giving everything to Jesus so that others could be set free and His will be done on earth. I remember realizing my own inability, seeking the Lord for and receiving a greater anointing, and consequently seeing more of the kingdom released through my life. There have also been various seasons where God brought about a greater measure of brokenness and humility. Though I can honestly say that progress has been made in many of these areas, I am well aware that I have a long way to go.

Just as the process of growing in Christ and in His ministry will be unique to each individual, the process of bringing about the brokenness that God desires will be unique as well. For Joseph it was betrayal by his brothers, false accusation, and time in prison. For Moses it was forty years in the desert. For David it was being under the leadership of King Saul who was jealous of him and constantly sought to take his life. For Peter it was his own failure in denying Christ that brought him to an end of himself. For Paul it was constant and harsh persecution.

There are various types of situations that help release a greater measure of brokenness into our lives. The primary theme in each of these scenarios is the same: *pain*. Pain will either produce brokenness or bitterness. When responded to and processed properly, pain and suffering will be the custom tools to form in us a deeper brokenness. When responded to poorly, the same pain and suffering will produce bitterness, coldness of heart, and unrighteous anger. It is very important that we submit to the processes that God brings us through with a proper attitude so that they will achieve the end that God has in mind. We cannot expect to walk in the power of Christ's resurrection while avoiding the fellowship of His sufferings.

Seasons of pain and confusion are unavoidable as we go through life. Times of disappointment will happen. Whether it is through the betrayal of family or close friends, persecution, misunderstanding, personal failure, false accusation, harsh authority figures, or other painful circumstances, let us submit to God in these seasons so that brokenness will be developed. As we embrace the cross, we will also experience the power of the resurrection. The result will be the fragrance of Christ being released through our lives.

The Value of Brokenness

As we have seen, brokenness is an integral part of God's process in our lives. Along with humility, it is one of those rare qualities that is hard to come by. More and more I have come to value this quality when I see it truly displayed in others. It is one thing to be a gifted minister and quite another to be a broken vessel.

God places tremendous value on brokenness. In fact, according to Isaiah 57:15 God's presence is attracted to the broken. Let's close this chapter by looking at a few other Scriptures on the subject.

But on this one will I look:
on him who is poor and of a contrite spirit,
and who trembles at My word. (Isaiah 66:2)

For You do not desire sacrifice, or else I would give it;
You do not delight in burnt offering.
The sacrifices of God are a broken spirit,
A broken and a contrite heart—
These, O God, You will not despise. (Psalm 51:16-17)

The Lord is near to those who have a broken heart,
And saves such as have a contrite spirit. (Psalm 34:18)

Blessed are the poor in spirit,
For theirs is the kingdom of heaven.
Blessed are those who mourn,
For they shall be comforted.
Blessed are the meek,
For they shall inherit the earth. (Matthew 5:3-5)

But we have this treasure in earthen vessels, that the excellence of the power may be of God and not of us. (2 Corinthians 4:7

10

Opposition to the Ministry of Jesus

Throughout this book, we have been talking about the ministry of Jesus and how we are to walk like Jesus walked. To be like Jesus is our aim. If we are to enter the fullness of the promises of God and the ministry of Jesus, we will have to do some contending. It will take focus, perseverance, and a willingness to go against the grain of the often-lukewarm Christianity that we find ourselves surrounded by today. No doubt, there will be many obstacles and much opposition.

Not everybody liked Jesus. You don't get crucified for simply being a nice guy. Jesus faced much opposition while ministering on earth, and He was a highly controversial figure. Some claimed He was the Messiah while others claimed that He was demon-possessed. Some said that He taught the truth while others said that He deceived the people. There was constant division as to who He really was, and even His own family did not believe in Him. He was constantly misunderstood; yet never felt the need to explain Himself. He was vehemently opposed; yet never defended Himself. Jesus had nothing to prove.

Anyone who dares to follow in the footsteps of Christ can expect similar controversy and resistance. There is as much opposition to the ministry of Jesus today as there was when He walked the earth. If we respond in the same manner as Christ—with humility and brokenness—we will help validate and advance His ministry today. If we respond with pride and bitterness, we can become a hindrance to it.

Opposing Leavens

In Matthew 13:33 Jesus said, "The kingdom of heaven is like leaven, which a woman took and hid in three measures of meal till it was all leavened." The kingdom of God is to have the same permeating effect in this world as leaven has in bread. But, the kingdom of heaven is not the only leaven that Jesus mentioned in the gospels. There are other leavens which oppose the ministry of Jesus and the influence of the kingdom of God.

> Then Jesus said to them, "Take heed and beware of the leaven of the Pharisees and the Sadducees." (Matthew 16:6)

> Then He charged them, saying, "Take heed, beware of the leaven of the Pharisees and the leaven of Herod." (Mark 8:15)

The above passages name a total of three opposing influences, or leavens: the Pharisees, the Sadducees, and Herod. It should be noted that although each one is different in nature, all three are warned against and must be guarded against by the people of God. I believe that the term *leaven* in the above passages refers to the teachings, mindsets, and overall spiritual influence that create a religious system. Possibly more dangerous than false religion is the perversion of true. Let's take a closer look at each of the three.

The Leaven of the Pharisees

The leaven of the Pharisees represents the teachings and mindsets of the Pharisees who were a strict religious sect of the Jews that were prominent in the days of Jesus. Along with another sect, the Sadducees, they fiercely opposed Jesus. It is very significant that the people who opposed the work of Christ most intensely were the religious leaders of the day. Today also, the biggest opponent of the work of the Holy Spirit in the earth is the religious systems that have been set up in much of the church.

The Pharisees could often be found testing Jesus with questions or interrogating those whom He had healed. The longest passage pertaining to this religious sect is found in Matthew 23 where essentially the whole chapter is given to Jesus' strong words of condemnation upon them. Based on this passage and several others that contain interactions with Jesus and the Pharisees, the Pharisees can be characterized in the following ways:

- Making painstaking efforts to appear righteous on the outside while neglecting inner purity. This equates to religious hypocrisy, evil pretending to be good.

- Giving lip service to God, while having a heart that is far away from Him

- Religious ritual that takes the place of true relationship with God

- Legalistic adherence to the law, without understanding the spirit of the law

- Zealously holding onto man-made traditions to the point of equating them with the Word of God (sometimes even *replacing* God's Word with tradition)

- A self-righteous, "holier than thou" attitude, especially towards the unlearned and/or sinners

- A total lack of compassion for those who are lost, hurting, and oppressed

- Weighing people down with religious rules, and being in control over others

- Love for money, recognition, and prominence among people

Even though we no longer have the religious sect of the Pharisees, the spirit (or leaven) of the Pharisees is alive and well. It is easy to point the finger at the religious leaders of Jesus' day, but how much are we influenced by the same leaven? While we must pursue a life of holiness and maintain doctrinal purity, we must also guard against the influence of the Pharisee spirit.

The influence of this religious leaven is manifesting itself in various forms in our churches today. In some cases, it is seen as a "form of godliness but denying its power" (2 Timothy 3:5). In this scenario there is a strong emphasis on correct doctrine while genuine experience with God and the power of the Spirit are severely limited. I am all for sound doctrine, but by itself, it is dead. I think of doctrine as being like the human skeletal system; absolutely necessary and yet not having life within itself. Christianity is a relationship, not a set of beliefs only. Again, we need sound doctrine, but doctrine is not an end in itself; it must lead us into knowing God Himself.

Another manifestation of the leaven of the Pharisees is legalism. This type of leaven influenced the early church when a group of Jewish believers known as the Judaizers tried to make gentile converts follow the Old Testament law. Paul sharply disputed this teaching, calling it a perversion of the gospel (see Galatians 1:7). This type of teaching is still around today, although it comes in different packages. In the name of holiness, many sincere believers get weighed down with legalistic rules that have more to do with outward appearance than inward purity. Legalism is especially dangerous when it deals with basing salvation on religious rules and form instead of repentance and saving faith in Jesus.

Another manifestation of this religious spirit is in the area of ritualism. In this case, spiritual disciplines like prayer and attendance at church become a ritual without any true life or meaning. They are done out of duty at best and guilt at worst. The denominations that are more liturgical, such as Catholic or Orthodox traditions, are often accused of this, but we in the Protestant church can be just as guilty.

And lastly, the leaven of the Pharisees can come in the form of traditionalism. This is where man-made traditions become equated with the Word of God and can sometimes even replace the commands of Scripture. We must not equate a style of worship, doctrinal bent, or man-made teaching with the clear commands of God's Word.

Jesus warned the disciples to be aware and guard against the leaven of the Pharisees. This deadly influence is a counterfeit to pure and genuine relationship with God and biblical Christianity. It empowers hypocrisy to thrive and allows darkness to go unchecked, covered by whitewashed tombs. Let's check our own hearts and ask the Lord to remove any remnant of this influence from our lives.

The Leaven of the Sadducees

The Sadducees were also an influential religious sect of the Jews in the time of Jesus. There are definitely some similarities between them and the Pharisees, but for the sake of our study it is more beneficial to look at their differences. Though the Bible gives less description of them, there are some key verses that tell us what to be on guard against.

In Matthew 22:23-33, a group of Sadducees questioned Jesus about the resurrection at the end of the age. (The Sadducees did not believe in the resurrection.) They made up a scenario in which a woman had been married to seven different brothers due to each one dying off, and then asked which one would be her husband in the resurrection. "Jesus answered and said to them, 'You are mistaken, not knowing the Scriptures nor the power of God'" (Matthew 22:29). Their approach to Jesus was very philosophical and basically came down to this: since we cannot understand the resurrection, it must not be true.

Another key passage is Acts 23:8: "For Sadducees say that there is no resurrection—and no angel or spirit; but the Pharisees confess both." Not only did the Sadducees not believe in the resurrection, they also denied the reality of the spiritual realm. It seems that they had a strong aversion to anything supernatural or miraculous. It is also important to understand that they did not accept the whole Old Testament as Scripture but only the first five books. While the Pharisees were sticklers for orthodoxy and the letter of the law, the Sadducees took a more academic approach.

With the above information, the Sadducees can be characterized as:

- Having a very naturalistic and philosophical world-view

- Denying portions of God's Word to be true Scripture

- Being highly skeptical about any type of supernatural activity

- Seeing God as a concept to understand rather than a Person to know and fellowship with

Over the last few hundred years, the leaven of the Sadducees has infiltrated huge segments of the church. This can primarily be seen in groups that we would call liberal in their theology. Many of the mainline denominations that started as true moves of the Spirit are now by and large so infected with the Sadducee leaven that they cannot be called Christian by biblical standards. Many universities that started as Christian training centers are now producing atheists who mock at the idea of the Bible being God's Word.

When a person tries to explain the miracles of the Bible in natural terms, the Sadducee spirit is at work. When the existence of demons is said to be a primitive, uneducated belief, again you have the influence of the Sadducees. Some even say that Jesus didn't believe in the existence of evil spirits but related to people's problems in that way in order to conform to the common belief of the time. It also is the leaven of the Sadducees that is behind ordaining homosexual clergy and behind a Universalist theology which says that everyone is going to heaven. The Sadducee leaven opposes such claims as the virgin birth, deity of Christ, and other fundamental doctrines of the faith.

Church history proves the devastating effects of this Sadducee leaven that Jesus warned His disciples about. Even though it cannot be seen as strongly in evangelical, Bible-believing Christianity, it is obvious that much that started out as evangelical has now become captive to this evil influence that opposes the truth of God's Word and the ministry of Jesus.

The Leaven of Herod

The meaning of the leaven of Herod is harder to pin down than that of the Pharisees and the Sadducees, because not much is stated about King Herod or the group called the Herodians in Scripture. We do know that the Herodians were a Jewish political party that supported King Herod. We see one instance of the Herodians working together with the Pharisees to trap Jesus in His words by asking Him a question about paying taxes (see Matthew 22:15-22). We also see that the Herodians and the Pharisees worked together to plot the death of Jesus (see Mark 3:6).

I believe that the key word which describes the leaven of Herod is political. Generally speaking, the leaven of the Pharisees is a *religious* spirit, the leaven of the Sadducees is a *philosophical* spirit, and the leaven of Herod is a *political* spirit. They are all unified in one thing: opposition to Jesus and His ministry. It is amazing that although the three groups typically hated each other, they were able to come together when it came to opposing the Messiah.

A while back I was praying and seeking insight from the Lord as to the nature of the political spirit, or leaven of Herod. Not long after that I came across the passage in Mark 15 where Jesus was on trial before Pilate. When I read verse 15, the Lord seemed to impress to me that this was a manifestation of the political spirit: "So Pilate, wanting to gratify the crowd, released Barabbas to them; and he delivered Jesus, after he had scourged Him, to be crucified." The key phrase is *wanting to gratify the crowd*. Isn't that a good description of many politicians? One of the biggest temptations for a politician is to compromise their standards in order to remain popular with the people. The leaven of Herod is a people-pleasing mindset.

To confirm this definition of the leaven of Herod, let's look at two other Scriptures. The first one refers to King Herod (Herod Antipas) who was responsible for the beheading of John the Baptist. Herod had put John into prison for preaching that he should not take his brother's wife, Herodias, to be his own. Herodias despised John for this and wanted to kill him, but since Herod feared John and considered him to be a holy man, he protected him (see Mark 6:20). One day at King Herod's birthday feast, Herodias' daughter pleased Herod with her dancing, and he offered to give her anything she wanted, up to half of his kingdom. After conferring with her mother, she requested the head of John the Baptist on a platter. Look at Mark 6:26: "And the king was exceedingly sorry; yet, because of the oaths and *because of those who sat with him,* he did not want to refuse her" (emphasis added). Like Pilate, who knew Jesus was innocent but gave into the crowd, Herod also was influenced by those who were with him.

The other Scripture is found in Acts 12 and refers to another King Herod, Herod Agrippa. In this context, Herod had just put the apostle James to death. Verse 3 says "And *because he saw that it pleased the Jews,* he proceeded further to seize Peter also" (emphasis added). Again, the motive was to please people and maintain popularity.

Based on the above Scriptures, here is my understanding of how the leaven of Herod is characterized:

- Primarily concerned with keeping people happy

- Not taking a strong stance on potentially controversial topics so that people on both sides of the issue are kept at ease

- Swayed by popular opinion instead of truth or convictions

- Willing to cater to the present desire in order to pacify people (in other words, a "chameleon")

The primary place that I see this political spirit influencing the church today is in what is known as the seeker-sensitive model of church growth. In an attempt to make the gospel or a church service more attractive to non-believers, various methods and techniques are used to ease a person into Christianity. In this type of church model, it is common to take surveys of both churched and unchurched people to figure out what people would like to see happen at church. Then, once you know what the people want, you give it to them.

This type of church model lends toward a performance and entertainment-based Christianity. The Sunday morning service is turned into a big event and a soulish show. Churches are built on human personality and charisma instead of on the pattern of the Word and power of the Spirit. God's presence is no longer seen as the top priority.

I have seen this leaven infect formerly Spirit-filled churches with devastating results. While numbers may increase, the move of the Holy Spirit is quenched. Convicting messages are no longer preached, prayer is pushed aside, and altar calls are removed. The gifts of the Spirit are not permitted to function in services, deliverance is not allowed, and the baptism of the Holy Spirit can only happen in separate meetings outside of the church gathering. This approach is an insult to the Spirit of God and a grave compromise. While we should all want to reach people with the gospel, using worldly methods to reach this goal should never be an option.

Another manifestation of the political spirit is a territorial attitude which is a result of building one's own kingdom instead of God's. I have been shocked to hear the way some pastors refer to other churches as if they were in competition with them. (These types of comments happen behind closed doors, because it would look bad to the public.) The political spirit turns the pastor into a CEO, the local church into a business, the saints into customers, and other churches into competition. Whose kingdom are we building?

Common Threads

As stated before, the Pharisees, Sadducees, and Herodians generally hated each other. They were unified in their opposition to Jesus however. Something about Jesus was a threat to them. Jesus didn't bow to their religious structure or political power. Jesus set the common people free, people who were formerly controlled by the religious system being perpetuated generation after generation.

We've looked at their differences, but I want to briefly point out some things that all three of these opposing leavens have in common. First, all three leavens are man-centered instead of Christ-centered. As subtle as it may be, self is placed on the throne instead of God. Whether it is self-righteousness, self-promotion, or self-importance, it is still just that: self! They are also man-centered in that they are ruled by the fear of man instead of the fear of God.

Secondly, all three have in common that they oppose the true work of the Holy Spirit. For example, the leaven of the Pharisees may oppose the gifts of the Spirit for religious reasons: "They ceased with the completion of Scripture." The leaven of the Sadducees opposes them for philosophical reasons: "We don't believe in that primitive supernatural stuff." Meanwhile, the leaven of Herod opposes the gifts for political, or people-pleasing, reasons: "We don't want the gifts to operate in the service, because it may offend somebody." In the end, the enemy's goal is accomplished: the Spirit is not moving and the ministry of Jesus is severely limited.

Another common thread is that in all three systems people are drawn to a church instead of to Christ. There will certainly be talk of Jesus and relationship with God, but the overall emphasis, whether subtle or obvious, will be connection to the particular church instead of to God Himself.

Finally, all three have in common that where they are allowed to have influence, they cause bondage and oppression to the people of God. Again, this will manifest in different ways with each one; it may be condemnation, manipulation, or intimidation but in the end it is bondage. Each of these three systems attempts to exert control over God's people, and God is saying "Let my people go!"

The Leaven of the Kingdom

In contrast to all of this is the leaven of the kingdom of God. Remember that in Matthew 13:33 Jesus said, "The kingdom of heaven is like leaven." A believer, church, or ministry that is filled with the leaven of the kingdom can be characterized in the following ways:

- Grounded in the whole counsel of God's Word

- Welcoming the full manifestation of the Holy Spirit in His fruit, gifts, and power

- Centered on Christ, His finished work on the cross, and His headship over the church

- Seeking unity in the body of Christ

- Prioritizing relationships; relationship with God first and then with people

- True freedom in Christ

The church was meant to be a living, relational organism and when the leaven of the kingdom has primary influence, that is what it will be. This organic nature can be seen in another way that Jesus described the kingdom: a mustard seed that grew into a large tree (see Matthew 13:31-32). The other leavens turn the church into a dead, mechanical organization. Making the church into a machine is a temptation, because you can force a machine to grow; a tree on the other hand has to grow at its own pace as it receives its proper nutrients and sunlight. The difference between a machine and a plant is that a plant has actual life and produces fruit while a machine is dead and has no power to bring forth fruit.

Where the leaven of the kingdom is growing, the ministry of Jesus has a place to flourish. This is because the message of the kingdom and the ministry of Jesus go hand-in-hand. The message of the kingdom preceded Christ's earthly ministry, and it prepares the way for it today as well. The main opposition to the ministry of Jesus will come from the three opposing leavens operating *within the church*, while the message of the kingdom paves the way for His ministry to operate.

Many believers find themselves unsatisfied with their church experience knowing that there must be something more. They hope and pray for change and even try to be change agents within their church. The problem is if you are a kingdom-minded person in a system other than the kingdom, you will constantly end up running into a wall of opposition. Unless there is a major spiritual overhaul starting with the leadership, there is little hope for any true change.

I often hear people say, "There is no such thing as a perfect church," and this is true. But there is a big difference between an imperfect church that is following after the kingdom and an imperfect church that is infiltrated by the spirit of the world. As long as at its core a church is kingdom-oriented and is committed to growing up in Christ, areas of immaturity are not a major cause for concern. It is not a matter of finding a perfect church but of finding one that's primary influence is the leaven of the kingdom and not the other three leavens.

Satan and the Leaven

Before Jesus ever faced any opposition from man, he had a face-to-face confrontation with the devil himself. Directly after being anointed by the Spirit and before He began His public ministry, Jesus went into the wilderness for forty days to be tested by the devil. As I was writing this chapter, I noticed something for the first time: the three temptations that Jesus overcame directly correlate to the three leavens that we have just discussed. I know that much could be said about each of the temptations apart from any discussion of the leavens, but I want to show how they relate so that we can understand the satanic origin of each of the three leavens. Let's take a look at the first two temptations together, and then we'll address the third.

Then Jesus was led up by the Spirit into the wilderness to be tempted by the devil. And when He had fasted forty days and forty nights, afterward He was hungry. Now when the tempter came to Him, he said, "If You are the Son of God, command that these stones become bread." But He answered and said, "It is written, 'Man shall not live by bread alone, but by every word that proceeds from the mouth of God.'" Then the devil took Him up into the holy city, set Him on the pinnacle of the temple, and said to Him, "If You are the Son of God, throw Yourself down. For it is written:

' He shall give His angels charge over you,'

and,
' In their hands they shall bear you up,
Lest you dash your foot against a stone.'"
Jesus said to him, "It is written again, 'You shall not tempt the Lord your God.'" (Matthew 4:1-7)

In the first test, Jesus is tempted to doubt the Word of God. Why do I say that? Well, the devil said, "*If* you are the Son of God..." (Matthew 4:3, emphasis added). If you jump back just three verses to Matthew 3:17 you will find that God had just spoken the words, "This is My beloved Son, in whom I am well pleased." So the temptation was a direct attack on the very thing that God had just said. Satan tried to plant a seed of doubt, similar to the first recorded words uttered by the serpent in the Garden of Eden, "Did God really say?" (see Genesis 3:1 NIV). This temptation therefore, relates to the leaven of the Sadducees who, as we have seen, had a chronic doubting of the Word of God.

In the second test, instead of a temptation to doubt the Word, it is a temptation to misuse the Word. Satan actually quoted a Scripture from the Psalms to try to get Jesus to fall into his trap. Misuse of the Scripture is a prime symptom of the religious spirit, and this temptation therefore relates to the leaven of the Pharisees. While the Sadducees doubted the Word, the Pharisees used the Word for their own ends.

Let's take a look at the third and final temptation.

> Again, the devil took Him up on an exceedingly high mountain, and showed Him all the kingdoms of the world and their glory. And he said to Him, "All these things I will give You if You will fall down and worship me." Then Jesus said to him, "Away with you, Satan! For it is written, 'You shall worship the Lord your God, and Him only you shall serve.'" (Matthew 4:8-10)

This is certainly an appeal to political power and relates to the leaven of Herod. And the price for such power? Compromise at its highest form; bowing down to worship the devil. Jesus could have what He ultimately came for—the kingdoms of this world—if He would worship the devil. This would also allow Him to bypass the cross. Only the devil offers a crown without a cross. Thankfully, Jesus rejected the offer. But those who embrace the political spirit end up building their own empire through pleasing man, all at the price of compromising the Word of God.

Yes, behind the leaven of the Pharisees, the leaven of the Sadducees, and the leaven of Herod is Satan himself. This gives us all the more reason to head the words of Jesus to beware of the leaven!

11

Leading Like Jesus

The important role of leaders is seen throughout the Bible. In the Old Testament we see key individuals like Moses and Joshua, and then the priests and Judges, and finally the prophets and kings. In the New Testament we see what's referred to as the five-fold ministry: apostles, prophets, evangelists, pastors, and teachers. We also see other leadership roles such as elders and deacons.

I am aware that many who read this book will not necessarily be in an official leadership role in the church. However, the lessons throughout this chapter can still help each believer understand principles of how leadership in God's kingdom is meant to function. And the heart and dynamics of leading like Jesus can be applied to any area that you have influence in—not just leadership positions in a church. We can lead like Jesus in the home, workplace, civic arena, and beyond.

Through the Old Testament kings, we get a clear picture of the overarching role of leadership. We see that when righteous kings such as David and Josiah were in place, God's people prospered and generally followed Him. When wicked kings such as Manasseh and Ahab were on the throne, the whole nation would go astray and fall into judgment. The power of leadership can also be seen in the life of Joshua. Look at what it says in Judges 2:7: "So the people served the Lord all the days of Joshua, and all the days of the elders who outlived Joshua, who had seen all the great works of the Lord which He had done for Israel." The next several verses go on to say that after Joshua and the elders died, a generation arose who ended up rebelling against the Lord.

The point I am making is this: godly leadership produces godly people. Leaders have a huge influence on the overall condition of the body of Christ. The devil knows this better than anybody else, and therefore spends much of his efforts on influencing the influencers. If he can infect the leaders of a local church or ministry, he has now gained a pathway into the lives of those who are under their care. In the previous chapter, we discussed three leavens that oppose the kingdom of God and the ministry of Jesus: that of the Pharisees, the Sadducees, and Herod. Remember that the term leaven refers to teachings, mindsets, and overall spiritual influence that creates a religious system. Before we discuss leading like Jesus, I want to first show how these opposing leavens can manifest in leadership.

Leaven in the Leadership

Over the last two decades, I have been in various leadership roles in ministries and churches, including six years as a lead pastor. I am growing and learning and have much more maturing to attain in my leadership journey. One thing I have found is that *leadership is not for the faint of heart*. It involves suffering, pain, and much perseverance. Indeed, I could write an entire book on the agonizing circumstances that my wife and I have walked through over the years. This is certainly not meant as a complaint; leadership has also been incredibly rewarding, and Jesus is worthy of our lives laid down in service to His people. While this chapter will call leaders to the high standards of Scripture and the model of Jesus, we should not be nitpicky toward leaders or expect perfection from them. Leaders are human and in a process like everyone else—they need much grace. At the same time, the leavens that Jesus warned about should not be tolerated in our churches and ministries as they are the antithesis of the nature of God's kingdom.

I believe that when a leader is unhealthy, unbroken, insecure, or prideful, it opens the door for the wrong leaven to come into their lives and then into their churches or ministries. When any of these three opposing leavens has a prominent place in a church, you can expect the role of leadership to be perverted. Leaders become oppressive task-masters, professional CEOs, entitled celebrities, or two-faced politicians. Some are well-meaning but caught up in a system that promotes unhealth and dysfunction. Others are wolves in sheep's clothing who use their position to prey on the flock (see Matthew 7:15).

One thing that leaders who are influenced by these leavens love is being in control. Whether it is control of the people or of the church service, this control ensures the security of the leader. It also greatly restricts the movement of the Holy Spirit and disempowers God's people. This control can take the form of intimidation, manipulation, or other tactics. It causes people to fulfill their religious obligations out of fear and guilt instead of faith and passion. While there is certainly a need for order and guidelines in any church or ministry, we are never meant to control the people of God or restrict the Holy Spirit's movement in our gatherings.

Another characteristic of leadership in these systems is giving more attention to people who are perceived to have charismatic personalities, wealth, or influence in society. It is amazing how easily we can cater to the ones who we think will help build our kingdom. This type of partiality is clearly exposed and condemned in the book of James (see James 2:1-9) and is a symptom of emphasizing outward appearance to inward realities.

Focusing attention only on the ones of certain wealth and status leads to a neglect of those who are in desperate need of ministry. The priest and the Levite in the parable of the Good Samaritan walked right past the man on the side of the road who was wounded and left for dead (see Luke 10:25-37). I used to always apply this famous parable to the need to feed the homeless and take care of orphans and widows. While that certainly does apply, the Lord has shown me a different perspective. What if the man lying on the side of the road bleeding is not a homeless person but a church member? I have come to realize that many in the church today are in the same condition spiritually as that man was physically. They've been stripped of all dignity, bruised and beaten, lied to and robbed by the devil, and left for dead. And the sad part is, the church usually has no real hope or answers for them.

Why did the priest and the Levite ignore the man? For various reasons I suppose. For one, they did not want to get their hands dirty. Secondly, they were on a journey; they were going somewhere, moving forward, and didn't have time for the man. And thirdly, they didn't want to incur any personal cost to themselves, with little chance for any return on investment. The Samaritan on the other hand gave the time, energy, and financial provision necessary to see the man healed and restored. He got his hands dirty, personally applying the oil and the wine, and didn't move forward with his journey until he was assured that the man would be taken care of.

My wife and I have ministered to individuals who were like the man on the side of the road. For the most part they are believers who have been actively involved in church for years. They needed deliverance from evil spirits as well as emotional healing, and many have been victims of various types of abuse. I wonder how many times they had been passed by.

Anytime that programs are prioritized over people, you can be sure that a leaven other than that of the kingdom is at work. The influence of the three leavens causes leaders to ignore the weak and wounded, because in these systems time, energy, and resources are only invested in those who will benefit the personal kingdom of the leader. If this seems like a harsh statement, consider the word of the Lord through Ezekiel the prophet to the leaders of his day.

> And the word of the Lord came to me, saying, "Son of man, prophesy against the shepherds of Israel, prophesy and say to them, 'Thus says the Lord God to the shepherds: "Woe to the shepherds of Israel who feed themselves! Should not the shepherds feed the flocks? You eat the fat and clothe yourselves with the wool; you slaughter the fatlings, but you do not feed the flock. The weak you have not strengthened, nor have you healed those who were sick, nor bound up the broken, nor brought back what was driven away, nor sought what was lost; but with force and cruelty you have ruled them.'" (Ezekiel 34:1-4)

The sheep were only used for personal gain. They were not cared for, fed, healed, or restored. These sobering words ring just as true today as they did in Ezekiel's day. Passages like this should cause every pastor and church leader to examine their own heart and determine if they are leading with purity of motive. Leadership is never for selfish purposes. It is a weighty responsibility to lead God's people—they belong to Him and must never be used or abused. A position of spiritual authority is for the purpose of feeding others, not feeding ourselves.

How Did Jesus Lead?

Throughout this book, we have covered the four main facets of the ministry of Jesus: preaching, teaching, healing, and deliverance. I have also emphasized the importance of intimacy with God, walking in compassion and brokenness, and the need for both authority and power. But it is also necessary to highlight the leadership of Jesus. In contrast to the shepherds in Ezekiel's day, Jesus showed a different way of leading. It carries authority with humility, sacrifice, and love. Its goal is not to take from the sheep but to give to the sheep. It is the way of self-sacrifice for the benefit of others.

Jesus referred to Himself as the Good Shepherd who lays down His life for the sheep. When the wolf comes, the hireling runs away, and the sheep are destroyed and scattered. That is because hirelings are not willing to pay the price of leadership. They are in it for personal gain, influence, power, money, and other benefits. They want the title and the authority without the responsibility. When it comes down to it, they don't really care about the sheep (see John 10:11-15). All who lead God's people must carefully determine whether they are leading in the order of the Good Shepherd or of the hireling. Are we willing to get our hands dirty? Are we willing to stand in harms way in order to protect the flock? Are we in it for ourselves or for God and His people?

When I look at the way Jesus led from an overarching perspective, three components stand out. *Jesus ministered to the multitudes, invested in the twelve, and was willing to stop for the one.* He had a broad impact. Sometimes He would teach thousands at a time. He would bring healing and deliverance to the masses. People were often flocking to Him in large numbers. But in the midst of all of this, He was very intentional to invest in a small group of future

154

leaders. And He was often seen stopping for individuals in need. These second two components are critical to leading like Jesus.

Jesus was intent on making disciples, not simply reaching masses. He gathered the twelve to Himself with the express purpose of walking with them and equipping them to do the very things He was doing (see Mark 3:13-15). This took time, energy, and great effort. But think of the long-term impact of this investment. With the exception of Judas who betrayed Him, what Jesus poured into the twelve went on to launch the early church and is still bearing eternal fruit to this day! Jesus multiplied His ministry through a discipleship process that was multi-faceted. There was relational connection, modeling and demonstrating, teaching and instructing, imparting, and giving opportunity to step out and apply what they were learning. As we lead in our spheres of influence, we should seek to incorporate these same facets as we pour into others as well. We should look for others to intentionally invest in and raise up.

I think it is worth mentioning here that we should not have unrealistic expectations of leaders in regards to their relational connection to the people they serve. Jesus did not have the same level of relationship with everyone. He specifically invested in His twelve apostles far more than other relationships, and even among the twelve it seems clear that He was closer to Peter, James, and John than the others. It is impossible to be closely connected to a large number of people, as we all have a limited amount of time and capacity. However, what we see in Jesus is that His style of leadership was relational, not mechanical. He cared more about His disciples' personal well-being, relationship with God, and character than in driving them to fulfill tasks. Relationship came before assignment.

What about stopping for the one? We see many examples of this in the ministry of Jesus. Whether it was a leper in need of healing, the woman who had the issue of blood, the man with the legion of

demons, or the blind man on the side of the road, we see Jesus willing to slow down and take time for an individual. He ministered to
those who could do nothing for Him in return. It is critical to always
keep this in mind: *we are never above stopping for the one*. While we
can't meet every need, we must never think we are too important
to stop for individuals. If we are to lead like Jesus, we must not only
minister to large groups but also pour into others and be willing to
take time for individuals.

The Heart of Kingdom Leadership

What Jesus modeled in His leadership He was careful to pass
on to His disciples. The following exchange gives great insight into
the heart and nature of a kingdom leader.

> But Jesus called them to Himself and said to them, "You
> know that those who are considered rulers over the Gen-
> tiles lord it over them, and their great ones exercise author-
> ity over them. Yet it shall not be so among you; but who-
> ever desires to become great among you shall be your
> servant. And whoever of you desires to be first shall be
> slave of all. For even the Son of Man did not come to be
> served, but to serve, and to give His life a ransom for
> many." (Mark 10:42-45)

A primary word that should be used to describe leaders in the
kingdom of God is *servants*. Jesus contrasts leadership in His kingdom with leadership in the world and shows that they are drastically different. Here is the paradox of God's leadership paradigm:
*In the world, people serve their leaders. In the kingdom, leaders serve their
people.* Those without a servant's heart are not qualified to be a
leader in the kingdom of God, no matter how great their gifting.
Jesus gave us the perfect example of what a true leader in the kingdom is to be like: He washed His disciples' feet and ultimately laid
down His life.

Pastors and other leaders in the body of Christ are not to lord their authority over people but instead are to use their position of influence to serve. This does not negate the reality of leadership authority but shows the heart-posture with which leadership authority is to be exercised in God's kingdom. Jesus is not promoting weak or passive leadership; He is expounding on the heart of leadership from God's perspective. Leadership, in its essence, is not about position or title. It is a function, a calling, a responsibility. The favor, anointing, and authority that God gives us is not for our own benefit but for the glory of God and the benefit of the ones we serve. The heart of leadership in the kingdom of God is to lay down our lives for the sake of others.

Again, it is not that leaders do not have authority. But they should never use that authority for selfish ends or to control others. It is up to the people to choose to submit to the authority of a leader; a kingdom-minded leader never demands such submission. This kind of selfless servanthood requires true humility. As leaders in God's kingdom, we must learn to humble ourselves and put the interests of others before our own. After all, the nature of a true servant is to be others-focused. Jesus said that whoever exalts himself will be humbled, and whoever humbles himself will be exalted (see Matthew 23:12). Whatever is produced through self-promotion will ultimately be brought down, but whatever is birthed in meekness and humility will be exalted by the Lord himself.

Foundations for Healthy Leadership

Not only is leadership much more than a position or a title, it is also not confined to methods and principles. More than leadership principles, theories, and models, healthy leadership comes from the *interior life* of an individual. This is so important to understand and live by. Heart, character, motivations, mindsets, and internal convictions all influence the way that we lead. If our interior life is not healthy, we cannot possibly lead in a healthy way. This is why God often works inside of us before He works outside of us.

We are exhorted in Proverbs 4:23, "Keep your heart with all diligence, for out of it spring the issues of life." Whatever is being cultivate inwardly will ultimately make its way out of us through our words and actions into the areas of influence that we have stewardship over. If there is confusion, jealousy, pride, bitterness, or selfish ambition in our hearts, these attributes will begin to take root in our areas of responsibility. If we are cultivating the fruit of the Spirit, these characteristics will permeate the environment in which we lead. Make no mistake: leadership starts on the inside.

There are great principles of leadership that we can learn and grow in—effective communication, decision-making principles, team-building, navigating transition, and so forth. These are helpful, and we should desire to improve our leadership skills in these ways. But these must be built on the proper foundation. I want to briefly cover three foundations for healthy leadership.

1. Intimacy

True leadership flows out of our relationship with God. If we do not keep intimacy with the Lord as our highest aim, we can easily get off track. Jesus modeled this for us perfectly. In the midst of intense ministry demands, He always took the time to get away and be alone with the Father. "However, the report went around concerning Him all the more; and great multitudes came together to hear, and to be healed by Him of their infirmities. So He Himself often withdrew into the wilderness and prayed" (Luke 5:15-16).

Leadership places many demands upon us, but we must not succumb to the temptation to neglect our personal walk with God. All genuine fruitfulness in God's kingdom comes from intimacy with the Lord. The most dangerous thing a leader can do is neglect their personal relationship with God.

2. Identity

Secondly, we must be secure in our identity. In a general sense, we must know who we are in Christ, be rooted in God's love as a son or daughter, and find our security in Him. We must not allow our ministry or leadership assignment to become the foundation of our identity, or we will lead from a place of insecurity.

We must also gain internal clarity about the specifics of our identity. Your unique personality, gifts, calling, testimony, and experiences will all come into play in how you lead. John the Baptist knew exactly who he was and who he wasn't (see John 1:19-28). If we do not know who we are, we will spend our lives trying to be everybody else. We must lead out of who we are.

3. Integrity

Psalm 78:72 says this about the leadership of King David: "So he shepherded them according to the integrity of his heart, and guided them by the skillfulness of his hands." Notice both internal and external factors in leadership. Integrity of heart is the internal reality, and skillfulness of hands is the external ability to lead. But integrity of heart must come first. To have integrity means to be a whole person. It means that who you are in secret is the same as who you are in public. It means that you do not have hidden sin or impure motives. It means that you have character and walk in holiness of heart, action, and speech. Here is an integrity check for me as a preacher: *Who I am in secret is more important than who I am in the pulpit. How I treat my wife and kids is more significant than how I am perceived from the platform.*

Leaders, who we are is more important than what we do. We must prioritize our relationship with God above all else. We must be rooted in a healthy identity in Christ. We must cultivate an interior life of holiness and integrity. Without these foundations, we will not be able to sustain healthy leadership over the long haul.

Leading as Fathers and Mothers

As we embrace the heart and mindset of leadership in God's kingdom and as we cultivate our inward life, we will be able to lead in ways that glorify God and bless His people. One of the ways we will see this expressed is through those who carry a true father's or mother's heart. The apostle Paul stated that the church in Corinth had many instructors but not many fathers (see 1 Corinthians 4:15). Unfortunately, this pattern holds true today. There are many teachers and leaders—there are few fathers.

What are some characteristics of fathers and mothers that are also traits of kingdom leaders? One is reproduction. Kingdom leaders reproduce their ministry in others. They have sons and daughters in the faith whom they are raising up and mentoring who will partake of the anointing that rests upon them. They birth others into ministry and release them into their gifts and calling, wanting their spiritual children to go beyond what they themselves have accomplished. When this is done correctly, spiritual children are not clones. They have their own unique identity, calling, and ministry expression. But they receive an inheritance that propels them far beyond what they could walk in apart from the relationship with a spiritual father or mother.

Another characteristic is relationship. Kingdom leaders are relational, not mechanical. This type of leadership is clearly seen with Christ who spent much time with the twelve disciples, calling them to be with Him before sending them out to minister (see Mark 3:14). There are certainly elements of correction involved, but correction is much easier to receive in the framework of a loving relationship. Expecting the ones under your leadership to produce results without a mentoring and nurturing relationship is like Pharaoh asking the Israelites to make bricks without straw, for it is in the context of genuine relationships that fruit is produced in the kingdom of God.

And finally, true fathers and mothers lead by example and so must leaders in God's kingdom. After Paul reminded the church at Corinth that he was their spiritual father he said, "Therefore I urge you, imitate me" (1 Corinthians 4:16). Paul was leading by his example, not just by his preaching. And since he was imitating Christ, he could ask others to imitate him. Jesus too led by example. He demonstrated the life that He preached about and only asked His followers to do things that He Himself was already doing.

True fathering and mothering in the church is rare, because it is costly. It has nothing to do with controlling others but instead sacrificially investing in them with no strings attached. It takes a willingness to spend and be spent for the sake of sons and daughters (see 2 Corinthians 12:14-15). While the cost is great, the reward is greater. But only those who are secure as sons and daughters of God can pour themselves out as fathers and mothers to others.

Shepherds of God's People

One of the words used for leaders throughout the Bible is *shepherds*. As Jesus is the Good Shepherd, His leaders are to follow in His footsteps in caring for His flock. In speaking to elders, Peter exhorts leaders to "Shepherd the flock of God which is among you, serving as overseers, not by compulsion but willingly, not for dishonest gain but eagerly; nor as being lords over those entrusted to you, but being examples to the flock" (1 Peter 5:2-3). Again, we see that purity of motive and a servant's heart is emphasized, along with leading by example.

As shepherds, leaders are to feed, lead, and protect the flock. Leaders nourish the people of God with the milk, bread, and meat of the Word. They also give wise counsel and instruction. They oversee and lead with clarity, vision, and direction, following the voice of the Chief Shepherd. And they protect the flock from false doctrine, spiritual attack, and wolves who come to devour. Paul encouraged the elders of Ephesus to be faithful in their role to shepherd the church and also warned them of wolves who would seek to bring harm and division (see Acts 20:28-31). This is a reality that we must not be ignorant or naïve about.

There are times as shepherds when we must use our authority to protect the flock. I remember one situation when I first became the lead pastor of our congregation. There was a man who started attending, and he was very quick to give prophetic words to people and seemed gifted in this area. But myself and others noticed a pattern of him cornering women and sharing words with them in a way that made them uncomfortable. Something seemed off and some women expressed concern. I decided to reach out to him and sit down for coffee. In the meantime, I contacted the previous ministry he was a part of and found out that they had asked him to stop giving prophetic words, because he was showing what appeared to be predatory behavior and making women feel uneasy.

While I did not have enough information to make a strong judgment such as removing him completely from our church, I knew that something needed to be done. So, I gave him a simple and reasonable boundary to see how he would respond. After some conversation with him, I asked him to simply come to our church for the next few months and be a part of the congregation without giving anyone prophetic words. Then, if he wanted to step into more ministry, he could look into joining our prayer ministry team. He accused me of being controlling and stopped attending! As a shepherd, I had to be willing to be misunderstood in order to protect the flock from potential harm. And sometimes, simple boundaries like the one in this example can go a long way in guarding the flock.

Over the years I have been involved in various situations where action was needed to protect the people of God. We must always walk in love and guard against making false accusations or walking in a harsh spirit when dealing with these types of scenarios. But when a person shows an ongoing pattern of deception, hypocrisy, abuse, predatory behavior, or aberrant teaching, shepherds must act to protect the flock.

Builders and Soldiers

Not only are leaders in the kingdom servants, fathers/mothers, and shepherds, but they are also *builders*. The Bible says that one of the reasons for leaders in the kingdom is "for the equipping of the saints for the work of ministry, for the edifying of the body of Christ" (Ephesians 4:12). This speaks both of building up individuals ("equipping the saints") and the church as a whole ("edifying the body of Christ"). Kingdom leaders know how to build people up, causing spiritual growth in the lives of those entrusted to them. Their focus is on building people not programs, and they build others up through praying, preaching, and pouring into them. They want to equip and empower others to do the ministry, and they are secure enough to release others into their gifts.

As stated above, these kingdom builders not only build up individuals but also the church as a whole. In 1 Corinthians 3:10, Paul described himself as a wise master builder and then gave some key instructions about building the church. The first key is that Jesus Christ Himself is the only true foundation. It is imperative that we build upon the foundation of Christ; His life, ministry, finished work on the cross, commands, and so forth. Secondly, as leaders build on the foundation of Christ, they can build using either gold, silver, and precious stones, or wood, hay, and straw (see verse 12). The emphasis here is clearly on quality. In an effort to grow quickly we must not resort to building the church with cheap substitutes that will only burn up at the judgment.

All leaders should remember that "Unless the Lord builds the house, they labor in vain who build it" (Psalm 127:1). It is Christ Himself who builds His church; leaders in the kingdom simply allow Him to do it through them. We can build a pretty successful looking church apart from the Lord, but in the end, it will be in vain. It is time to allow Jesus to build His church according to His pattern.

And a final word to describe leaders in the kingdom of God is *soldiers*. This speaks of the character, discipline, and perseverance required to effectively lead God's people. Paul told Timothy that he "must endure hardship as a good soldier of Jesus Christ" (2 Timothy 2:3) and when he outlined the requirements for leadership in the books of 1 Timothy and Titus, he made it abundantly clear that character and integrity are a must. Character is developed over time, and kingdom leaders submit to God's process of refining in order to have Christ's character and nature formed in them so that their ministry is not undermined by hypocrisy or sin.

Like soldiers, kingdom leaders are disciplined. They live a lifestyle of prayer and fasting and have a single-minded focus on their calling. Paul also compares this type of discipline to athletic training which further demonstrates the type of focus and determination required for leadership. What separates average athletes from great athletes is not talent but consistent training and a disciplined lifestyle that centers around the particular sport that they are involved in.

Perseverance is also a mark of a good soldier and of leaders in the body of Christ. They press through obstacles and opposition and run the race with endurance. Anyone can start in a marathon but only those with perseverance can finish it. Likewise, kingdom leaders do not give up when things get difficult but have learned to persevere through the storms and pressures of life and ministry.

Five-Fold Ministry

Now that we have looked at the nature of leaders in the kingdom, let's look at some particular types of leaders. "And He

Himself gave some to be apostles, some prophets, some evangelists, and some pastors and teachers, for the equipping of the saints for the work of ministry, for the edifying of the body of Christ." (Ephesians 4:11). When Jesus ascended to the right hand of the Father, He gave gifts to the church, and these are often known as the five-fold ministry gifts. It is worth noting that these are not of the same nature as the manifestation gifts of the Spirit listed in 1 Corinthians 12. In 1 Corinthians 12 the gifts are manifestations of the Spirit given to individuals. In Ephesians 4 the gifts are individuals given to the church as a whole. Do you see the difference? In 1 Corinthians 12 a person may operate in or have a gift, but in Ephesians 4 the person *is* the gift. It is also important to mention that these five-fold ministry gifts are not titles but functions and callings. In an attempt to restore these ministries, we must not succumb to the temptation to become obsessed with titles. Jesus warned us that that is how the Pharisees of His day operated (see Matthew 23:6-7).

Each of the five ministry gifts is actually a facet of the ministry of Jesus Himself, and they are given to the church so that it will be equipped and come to maturity. One of the absolutely crucial elements to restoring the ministry of Jesus is a full restoration of all of the five-fold gifts to the church. In the following paragraphs I will give a brief description of each of the five gifts primarily for the purpose of highlighting their basic functions and differences, while relating them to the ministry of Jesus.

Apostle

The Greek word that is translated as *apostle* means "one who is sent forth." An apostle is someone who is sent by God to represent Jesus and to advance and establish the kingdom of God on earth. They are entrusted with tremendous spiritual authority and must therefore walk in deep humility. They operate in the miraculous, casting out demons and healing the sick. They are fathers/mothers who raise up sons and daughters, builders in the church who lead movements and establish order. An apostle must have a clear commissioning from the Lord Himself, and that calling must also be recognized by a local body. One of the best examples of this in the book of Acts is when Paul and Barnabas were sent from Antioch (see Acts 13:1-4). Before this event, they were functioning as teachers and/or prophets in the local church, but after being sent out they were referred to as apostles (see Acts 14:14).

Did you know that Jesus was the first apostle? Hebrews 3:1 says, "Therefore, holy brethren, partakers of the heavenly calling, consider the Apostle and High Priest of our confession, Christ Jesus." Jesus is the ultimate example of an apostle being sent by the Father from heaven to earth to establish the kingdom of God.

Prophet

A *prophet* is one who receives and declares the heart and mind of God for individuals, churches, cities, nations, and the world. While all Christians can hear the voice of God and all Christians can operate in the gift of prophecy, a prophet specializes in these things and has a special calling to them. A prophet may receive revelation from God in many ways, but I would say that these ways can be placed into two primary categories: seeing and hearing. Seeing refers to having the eyes opened to see in the spiritual realm, as well as the area of dreams, visions, and trances. Hearing refers to the still small voice, internal voice, and audible voice of God. God uses prophets to make known His destiny to people as well as to churches, cities, and nations. He raises up prophets to call the people of God to repentance and restore the standard of holiness. Prophets release the plumbline of God's Word and turn people back to the Lord.

Prophetic ministry is essential in the body of Christ today, because not only do we need to be grounded in the Scriptures, we also need to know the heart and mind of God for the specific situations of our day. For instance, Agabus was a prophet in the early church and he prophesied of a severe famine that was coming, and thus the church was prepared when the famine came (see Acts 11:27-29). That kind of specific knowledge cannot be gained by studying the Bible but only through prophetic revelation. To be clear, no prophecy is equated to Scripture or added to the Bible. The Bible is the final authority for the church and any prophetic word that is from God will certainly be in line with it. But having the Bible does not mean that it is no longer necessary to have the gift of prophecy and the ministry of the prophet.

Jesus was certainly a prophet. He trumpeted the voice of God and also prophesied to individuals at times. One example of the prophetic ministry of Jesus is when He encountered the woman at the well and "read her mail," resulting in her coming to a knowledge of Jesus as the Messiah (see John 4:1-30).

Evangelist

An *evangelist* has one thing burning in their heart: reaching the lost with the gospel of Jesus Christ. They do this in two ways: reaching the lost themselves and equipping the church to reach them. Phillip, who was originally a deacon in the early church, is a great example of a New Testament evangelist. Acts chapter 8 shows him preaching the gospel to crowds of people in Samaria, seeing many turn to the Lord. His preaching was confirmed with miracles of healing and deliverance, and this drew the attention of the people. His ministry in Samaria is compared and contrasted to a local sorcerer named Simon. It is significant that the people had listened to and followed Simon for the same reason that they listened to Phillip: supernatural signs. But while Simon promoted himself, Phillip preached Christ. If we operate in signs and wonders people will listen; so we had better make sure that we are preaching the right message and bringing people to Christ and not ourselves.

In the same chapter we see that Phillip also reached a single individual, an Ethiopian eunuch, as the Spirit led him. This shows that people can be reached through large gatherings as well as one-on-one evangelism. In the end we need to remember that evangelism is the work of the Holy Spirit. Our job is to be led and empowered by the Spirit so that souls will be saved.

Jesus was an evangelist. He came preaching the good news to the poor. Evangelists today are an extension of His ministry to seek and save the lost.

Pastor

A *pastor* is responsible for the spiritual well-being of a particular group of believers. While the other four ministry gifts will probably travel and minister to the body of Christ as a whole, the pastor is primarily and essentially given to a local church. The word for pastor relates to the word shepherd. A pastor is one who has care for a flock and is responsible for leading, teaching, nurturing, correcting, and maintaining a long-term relationship with them.

It is important that local churches have true pastors in leadership. What I mean is this: it is possible, and actually quite common, for the pastor of a church to not be a five-fold pastor. Many lead pastors are actually evangelists, prophets, or teachers by nature even though they carry the title of pastor. I think that this is fine as long as there is someone in the leadership who is fulfilling the function of pastor to the flock. This is why team ministry is so important. Each of the five ministry gifts carries a different dimension of the ministry of Christ that the body of Christ needs in order to be healthy.

Jesus is the ultimate example of a pastor, calling Himself the Good Shepherd in John chapter 10. He selflessly put the needs of His sheep before Himself and gave His life for the flock.

Teacher

Teachers in the body of Christ are most concerned that the people of God become grounded in His Word. They have a deep love for the Bible and are great at explaining it in ways that people can understand. They interpret the Scriptures and teach with authority in both the fundamental areas as well as the more complex subjects of Christianity. Good teaching is so important, because it roots people in the Word of God. Every Christian should read the Bible on their own, but it is also important to receive ministry from those who are called as teachers to the body of Christ.

Acts 13:1 says that the church in Antioch had both prophets and teachers in its leadership. Generally speaking, prophets specialize in the *rhema* Word of God (revelatory spoken Word) while teachers focus on the *logos* Word of God (complete written Word), and both are vital to the Christian. This again shows the need for balance and team leadership in the church. If a church has only prophets, it will be constantly receiving prophetic words and revelations but will not be grounded in the Bible. If it has only teachers, it will be rooted in the truth of the Word that applies to all believers but will be lacking in the life-giving words that are specific to itself and its members that can release them into their destiny.

One of the most common titles for people to call Jesus was Teacher. Like I mentioned in Chapter Four, Jesus didn't just teach the letter of the law, He cut through to the spirit of the law. In the same way, teachers today are able to unpack the Word under the anointing of the Spirit and cause the people who hear to grow in Christ.

Are You a Saul or a Paul Type Leader?

Quite often, the leadership style of King Saul is compared to that of his successor, King David. There is much that can be learned from this comparison, but in bringing this chapter to a close, I felt prompted to instead compare King Saul to another man named Saul: Saul of Tarsus, better known as the apostle Paul.

King Saul started out well, while the apostle Paul started out as a violent persecutor of the church. By the end of their lives however, you would have never known that each one had started the way they did. Saul turned into a demonized madman whose life ended in complete disaster. Paul had a radical conversion and at the end of his life was able to say that he had fought the good fight and finished his race (see 2 Timothy 4:7). Let's compare these two leaders, drawing out their drastically different approaches to leadership. Saul represents leadership influenced by the leaven of the Pharisees, Sadducees, and Herod. Paul represents leadership in the kingdom of God.

The difference between King Saul and the apostle Paul can really be summed up in this one statement: Saul was consumed with the kingdom of Saul while Paul was concerned for the kingdom of God. While Saul set up a monument to himself, Paul set out to glorify Christ and establish His kingdom. These realities can be seen more clearly when we compare how each one treated those entrusted to their care.

Saul told David he was too young. Paul told Timothy, "let no one despise your youth." Sauls patronize while Pauls authorize. Saul placed his armor on David which led to restriction. Paul placed his hands on Timothy which led to empowerment. Sauls have a way of putting a ceiling above those under them that never allows them to blossom in their gifts but instead causes them to conform into something that does not really fit them. Pauls however, activate people into their gifts and release them into their destiny.

Because of insecurity, Saul was threatened by David's gifting and jealous of his accomplishments. Paul however constantly stirred up Timothy's gifts and encouraged him to complete his God-given assignment. Therefore, Saul sought to murder while

Paul sought to mentor. Saul chased David while Paul sent Timothy. Saul was known for throwing spears while Paul was known for shedding tears. Saul preyed upon David while Paul prayed for Timothy. Saul squeezed the life out of David while Paul poured his life into Timothy. Saul lorded like a pharaoh while Paul loved like a father.

The difference between the leadership of these two men is remarkable. Being in a position of authority is a tremendous responsibility and carries with it many temptations. Will we use our position to serve ourselves or to influence and serve others? To build up or tear down? To control or to release? To draw people to ourselves or to God? Those in leadership positions must constantly humble themselves before the Lord, seek His face, and ensure that they carry His heart as they lead His people.

12

The Gate of Heaven

Before Jesus was launched into His earthly ministry, a significant event took place. It is recorded in Matthew 3:16-17: "When He had been baptized, Jesus came up immediately from the water; and behold, the heavens were opened to Him, and He saw the Spirit of God descending like a dove and alighting upon Him. And suddenly a voice came from heaven, saying, 'This is My beloved Son, in whom I am well pleased.'"

Several years ago as I was reading this passage, I was drawn into the phrase *the heavens were opened to Him*. I had always emphasized that the Holy Spirit came upon Jesus and that the Father's blessing was released over Him. But I had glossed over the fact that when Jesus was baptized, the heavens opened up to Him. As I meditated on this concept, the Holy Spirit led me into a revelation on the topic of open heavens. I began to see just how important this event was in the life of Jesus. Everything that flowed out of His ministry started with this open heaven encounter.

We are called to walk like Jesus walked and do what Jesus did. But we can't do what Jesus did unless we have what Jesus had. He had intimacy with the Father, compassion for people, authority over the devil, and the power of the Holy Spirit. But He also had an *open heaven*.

What is an Open Heaven?

While this will only be a brief overview of the topic, I want to give some insight into what constitutes an open heaven. The concept is mentioned in various places throughout the Bible. We will look at an example in Genesis 28 a little later in the chapter, but here are a few other examples in Scripture.

> Now it came to pass in the thirtieth year...that the heavens were opened and I saw visions of God. (Ezekiel 1:1)

> Oh, that You would rend the heavens!
> That You would come down!
> That the mountains might shake at Your presence—
> As fire burns brushwood,
> As fire causes water to boil—
> To make Your name known to Your adversaries,
> That the nations may tremble at Your presence!
> (Isaiah 64:1-2)

> But he, being full of the Holy Spirit, gazed into heaven and saw the glory of God, and Jesus standing at the right hand of God, and said, "Look! I see the heavens opened and the Son of Man standing at the right hand of God!" (Acts 7:55-56)

After these things I looked, and behold, a door standing open in heaven. And the first voice which I heard was like a trumpet speaking with me, saying, "Come up here, and I will show you things which must take place after this." Immediately I was in the Spirit; and behold, a throne set in heaven, and One sat on the throne. (Revelation 4:1-2)

When the heavens are opened, God becomes *real*. The revelation of God, His kingdom, and eternal realities are released in powerful ways on earth. We go from the *concept* of God to the *reality* of God. From the *omnipresence* of God to the *manifest presence* of God. There are outpourings of the Holy Spirit, a harvest of souls, powerful miracles, healing, and deliverance. God's blessings are poured out and His righteous judgments are released. Barriers in the spiritual realm are removed, and the veil between heaven and earth is torn. There is access on earth to the riches stored in heaven.

I have heard some people say or imply that since the heavens were already opened for Jesus, they no longer need to be opened any more. It is believed that they are automatically opened because of what Jesus accomplished for us. To that I say: *show me the fruit*. In the Bible, open heavens have tangible evidence as seen in the passages quoted earlier and the descriptions in the previous paragraph. We must not settle for theological theories without experiential realities. Not to mention the fact that in the Scriptures, the heavens are opened up multiple times throughout the New Testament. It was not a once-and-done experience.

House of God, Gate of Heaven

The New Testament defines the church using various descriptions. We are the body of Christ, representing Him on earth, with various gifts and ministries functioning together in unity. We are the bride of Christ, walking in purity and intimacy with Him. We are the army of God, advancing His kingdom and tearing down the gates of hell. We are the family of God, living in community and love for one another. And we are also the house of God, the very dwelling place of God on earth.

> ...having been built on the foundation of the apostles and prophets, Jesus Christ Himself being the chief cornerstone, in whom *the whole building*, being fitted together, grows into a *holy temple* in the Lord, in whom you also are being built together for a *dwelling place of God* in the Spirit. (Ephesians 2:20-22, emphasis added)

As the house of God, we are also called to be the *gate of heaven* in the earth. Genesis 28 records an incredible dream that the patriarch Jacob had. Verse 12 says, "Then he dreamed, and behold, a ladder was set up on the earth, and its top reached to heaven; and there the angels of God were ascending and descending on it." The passage goes on to describe how the Lord appeared to Jacob at the top of the ladder and spoke to him confirming the covenant that had been made with Abraham and Isaac. Then we read the following: "Then Jacob awoke from his sleep and said, 'Surely the Lord is in this place, and I did not know it.' And he was afraid and said, 'How awesome is this place! This is none other than *the house of God*, and this is *the gate of heaven!*'" (Genesis 28:16-17, emphasis added).

When Jacob awoke from the dream, he was stunned at what he had seen and experienced. The heavens were opened up, bringing him into the immediate presence of God. God was already there, but now he *knew it*. Notice what he described the place as: *the house of God and the gate of heaven*. It is very significant that this is the first mention of the expression house of God in the Bible and that it is paired with the phrase gate of heaven. The house of God is the gate of heaven. The word gate speaks of an access point. In other words, the gate of heaven refers to heaven's entrance point into the earth. Jesus also spoke of the phrase gates of hell, which speaks of hell's

176

access points into the earth and into individual lives (see Matthew 16:18).

If the church is the house of God, and the house of God is the gate of heaven, then the church is the gate of heaven. What I am trying to say is this: *the people of God both individually and corporately are to be heaven's entrance point into the earth.* The church is the gate of heaven, or heaven's access point into this world. Jesus modeled this perfectly in His earthly ministry.

Jesus the Gate

Jesus made a clear connection to the gate of heaven early in His ministry. In John 1:51 He said, "Most assuredly, I say to you, here-after you shall see heaven open, and the angels of God ascending and descending upon the Son of Man." This is a definite reference to the dream that Jacob had in Genesis 28. Jesus was basically say-ing, "Remember that dream that Jacob had? Well, I am a fulfillment of that dream. The angels of God ascend and descend upon *Me*. I am the house of God and the gate of heaven; heaven enters into the earth through Me." Jesus came into this earth as the gate of heaven. We know that Jesus claimed to be the temple of God (see John 2:19-21) and as we have just seen, the temple or house of God is the gate of heaven.

Like Noah's dove, the Holy Spirit seeks a place to land on earth. When Jesus was baptized by John, the Dove found His resting place. "And John bore witness, saying, 'I saw the Spirit descending from heaven like a dove, and He *remained* upon Him'" (John 1:32, emphasis added). We already saw that in Matthew's version of Christ's baptism it says that the heavens were opened to Him. Jesus had full access to heaven while walking on earth. We are called to walk the same way. The Bible says that believers are seated with Christ in heavenly places and that our citizenship is in heaven (see Ephesians 2:6, Philippians 3:20). We are citizens of earth and citizens of heaven at the same time. We must learn to access heaven and release it into the earth.

We see throughout the Scriptures that God dwelt among His people. In the Old Testament He dwelt in the tabernacle and in the first and second temple. When Jesus came, He established a new order: God dwelling in His people. Jesus became the temple or dwelling place of God in the earth, and all who receive Him carry the same awesome privilege. But God not only wants to dwell in His people, He wants to be released through them into the earth. He wants to express His nature and power, and He looks for vessels to do it through. Jesus therefore not only became the dwelling place for God's presence, but as the gate of heaven became the means through which the Father expressed Himself to the world and manifested His kingdom.

Everywhere Jesus went, He released the resources of heaven to those around Him. When Jesus healed the sick and cast out demons, He was releasing heaven's power. When He fed the five thousand, He was releasing heaven's provision. And when He calmed the storm, He was releasing heaven's peace. As a *walking open heaven*, Jesus brokered heaven's resources. Today still there is no lack of power, provision, or peace on heaven's end, only a lack of entrance into the earth.

Your Kingdom Come

Many people believe that because He is sovereign, God's will automatically happens on the earth. This is illustrated by questions such as "Why doesn't God stop the hunger and poverty problems in the world?" or "Why doesn't God just get rid of all sickness?" The typical answer to these questions goes something like this: "Well, God is sovereign, and He sees from an eternal perspective so we just need to trust Him." Though there is a measure of truth in that answer, it is not the complete picture. It leaves the role that mankind plays in the affairs of this world out of the equation.

God is in fact sovereign but that does not mean that everything that happens on the earth is His will. He chose to give dominion over the earth to mankind, and He has worked within that framework ever since. It is not that God does not want to feed the hungry or heal the sick; it is that He can't seem to find enough people to do it through. This does not mean that God is not all-powerful or that He is weak in any way. In His sovereignty He has decided to work on the earth through people. Therefore, we must wake up to our responsibility to partner with Him in seeing His will accomplished. As the gate of heaven, we are to release His resources in the earth.

This responsibility is seen in the way that Jesus taught us to pray in Matthew 6:10: "Your kingdom come. Your will be done on earth as it is in heaven." There is no point in praying for God's will to be done on earth if this automatically happens. It is a misunderstanding of the sovereignty of God to say that His will automatically happens. As Christians we have given our allegiance to Jesus and have come under His rule and now have a mandate to demonstrate and advance His kingdom. We are ambassadors for His kingdom, contending for His rule and reign to be extended throughout the earth. Many people want the benefits of the kingdom without the rule of the King. But if you reject the King, you have no place in the kingdom. If we receive Him as King, we also receive His kingdom, with all that comes with it.

Our job is to make "on earth as it is in heaven" a reality. There is no sin in heaven, and therefore we preach the power of the cross to remove the penalty of sin and break its power from people's lives. There is no sickness in heaven, and therefore we see it as an enemy to be destroyed. There is no oppression or torment in heaven, and therefore we cast out demons and set captives free. There is no lack or hunger in heaven and so we clothe the naked and feed the hungry. Our role is to see souls saved, lives transformed, and heaven come to earth.

Becoming a Gate of Heaven

Jesus said that the kingdom of heaven is within us (see Luke 17:21). We must learn how to release this kingdom into the world around us.

How can we experience the reality of an open heaven over our lives, churches, and regions? How can we become a gate of heaven in the earth, releasing the resources of heaven wherever we go? There is certainly no formula for this, but I want to cover a few keys for seeing open heavens become a reality.

Tenacious Prayer

Prayer is one of the main vehicles that God has chosen to use in order to bring heaven to earth. In Luke's version of Jesus' baptism, it highlights the fact that the heavens were opened to Jesus *while He prayed* (see Luke 3:21). We also see that it was in the context of constant corporate prayer that the Holy Spirit was first poured out on the day of Pentecost. The Bible says that as the disciples waited for the promised outpouring, "They all joined together constantly in prayer, along with the women and Mary the mother of Jesus, and with his brothers" (Acts 1:14).

Church history shows that this is the pattern of every revival—constant prayer and then an outpouring of the Spirit. But in studying the history of past revivals, I have also noticed that the type of prayer that preceded outpourings of the Holy Spirit has been at a level and quality that few seem to be familiar with today. This type of prayer is characterized by almost unbearable prayer burdens, tears, groans, and travail. It is also accompanied by stubborn faith, unwavering persistence until the promise is fulfilled, and long seasons of waiting on the Lord. It reminds me of Elijah laboring in prayer until the heavens opened and poured out rain after years of drought (see 1 Kings 18:41-46). Make no mistake: *revival is not birthed through casual prayer.* The heavens don't open over the indifferent. We must press in with tenacity and faith until the outpouring comes.

The church is called to be a house of prayer, and when we give ourselves to prayer, we release the kingdom to come "on earth as it is in heaven." The practice of waiting on the Lord in prayer has become almost extinct in our day. We could do with far fewer planning meetings and many more prayer meetings, fewer strategy sessions and more seeking the face of God. We need intercession not just organization. Only the praying church can accurately be called the house of God, for His house is a house of prayer (see Matthew 21:13). To be the gate of heaven we must be the house of God, and to be the house of God, we must be a praying people. The Holy Spirit dwells and moves only among a people of prayer.

Not only is corporate prayer a way to release heaven on earth, but individual prayer is also a means for the kingdom to come. Prayer in the context of ministering to another person fulfills this purpose as well. When you pray over someone, whether inside the church or outside of it, you are giving the Holy Spirit a chance to move in a supernatural way. Every time you ask to pray for someone who needs healing for example, the Healer has an opportunity to establish His will.

Consecration and Obedience

Another key for open heavens is consecration and obedience. When Jesus stepped into the waters of baptism, it was an act of obedience to the Father. It was also a step toward the cross as He allowed Himself to be identified with sinful humanity. Jesus was without sin, but He was baptized along with sinners who were coming to confess and repent of sin. From this moment on, His life dramatically changed. Normal life was over, and He was moment by moment living to fulfill the Father's will in a new way. It was an act of complete consecration to God. His life was not His own.

Full consecration leads to fullness of the Spirit. It was Mary of Bethany going all in that released the fragrance in the room. As we give ourselves completely to Jesus, the fragrance of heaven will flow out of our lives. And when we step out in obedience to the commands of God, dramatic results can occur. Simple acts of obedience can release awesome acts of power. When Moses lifted up his staff in obedience to God, the Red Sea parted. When Joshua and his army marched around Jericho and then shouted at the top of their lungs, the walls crumbled to the ground. When Peter and his fishing partners obeyed the command of Jesus to launch out to the deep and let the nets down, so many fish were caught that the boat almost sank.

There have been times in deliverance sessions where small acts of obedience released the presence and power of God in profound ways. Once when a woman and I were ministering to a lady, the woman who was ministering with me felt led to give the one we were praying for a hug. She asked permission and then hugged her. As soon as she did, something broke. The Holy Spirit moved in a profound way and tears began to flow. A powerful deliverance took place that launched her forward into her walk with God. It's not that giving hugs is a formula for seeing people set free, it is that obeying the voice of God releases His presence and power. I could give many other similar examples.

When we step out in obedience to the commands of God—both in the Scripture and from the voice of the Holy Spirit—God's kingdom is released in the earth.

Releasing Testimonies

The final key I will mention is the sharing of testimonies. When many Christians hear the word *testimony*, they usually think of the story of how a person was saved. This is one example of a testimony but certainly not the only one. A testimony is to declare what God has done. It can be for salvation, healing, provision, deliverance, protection, and so forth. We should always have fresh testimonies of the goodness and power of God in our lives.

Releasing testimonies is powerful for a few reasons. For one, you cannot argue with a testimony. When Jesus healed a man who was born blind, the Pharisees got upset, because the miracle took place on the Sabbath. As they questioned the blind man he said, "Whether He is a sinner or not I do not know. One thing I know: that though I was blind, now I see" (John 9:25). You can't argue with that! Testifying to what God has done shows the world that God is real and cuts through people's arguments.

Testimonies are also powerful in that within each testimony is an invitation for others to step into what God has already done. When you testify about salvation, you invite others to be saved. When you testify about deliverance, you invite others to be set free. Testimonies ignite faith in others, and God delights to reproduce the miracle.

Will He Find You?

There are many other ways that God releases the kingdom of God through our lives. It can come through prophetic words, prophetic acts, acts of compassion, praise and worship, preaching, radical generosity, and many other means. The point is to release the kingdom of God so that His will can be done on earth as it is in heaven. Jesus said that the Holy Spirit would be like rivers of living water in the life of the believer (see John 7:37-39). The Spirit not only wants to dwell in us but also flow out of us to others.

Heaven is looking for an entrance into the earth, and believers are to be that entrance. We are the dwelling place of God and gate of heaven in the earth. Jesus modeled for us what the Christian life could be, and now we must see this as the goal and contend for the fullness of our inheritance in Christ. Healing the sick and casting out demons must become our normal experience and intimacy with God our highest goal.

Second Chronicles 16:9 says, "For the eyes of the Lord run to and fro throughout the whole earth, to show Himself strong on behalf of those whose heart is loyal to Him." God is searching the earth for people who have given complete allegiance to the King. He is looking for the consecrated ones, the hungry ones, the ones with undivided devotion to Him. Once He finds them, there is no limit to the love and power that He will display through their lives. As He finds more and more of these kingdom people, the ministry of Jesus is being restored to the earth.

The question is, will He find *you*?